What People are saying
about *Threshold Bible Study*

"Falling in love with the sacred Scriptures enables us to fall in deeper love with our loving God. *Threshold Bible Study* helps us see the Word of God alive in us and among us."
ARCHBISHOP GREGORY M. AYMOND, *Archbishop of New Orleans*

"With lucidity and creativity, Stephen Binz offers today's believing communities a rich and accessible treasury of biblical scholarship. The series' brilliance lies in its simplicity of presentation complemented by critical depth of thought and reflective insight."
CAROL J. DEMPSEY, OP, *Associate Professor of Theology, University of Portland, OR*

"*Threshold Bible Study* offers solid scholarship and spiritual depth. It can be counted on for lively individual study and prayer, even while it offers spiritual riches to deepen communal conversation and reflection among the people of God."
SCOTT HAHN, *Founder and President of the St. Paul Center for Biblical Theology*

"*Threshold Bible Study* is a terrific resource for parishes, groups, and individuals who desire to delve more deeply into Scripture and church teaching. Stephen J. Binz has created guides that are profound yet also accessible and that answer the growing desire among today's laity for tools to grow in both faith and community."
LISA M. HENDEY, *Founder of CatholicMom.com and author*

"Stephen Binz provides the church with a tremendous gift and resource in the *Threshold Bible Study*. This great series invites readers into the world of Scripture with insight, wisdom, and accessibility. This series will help you fall in love with the word of God!"
DANIEL P. HORAN, OFM, *Catholic Theological Union, Chicago*

"Stephen J. Binz has a unique talent for helping ordinary folks engage the Bible with deep understanding. Graduates of the Hartford Catholic Biblical School are using his *Threshold Bible Study* throughout Connecticut to bring Scripture more fully into the lives of God's people."
BJ DALY HORELL, *Director, Catholic Biblical School, Archdiocese of Hartford*

"*Threshold Bible Study* takes to heart the summons of the Second Vatican Council—'easy access to Sacred Scripture should be provided for all the Christian faithful' (*Dei Verbum*, #22)—by facilitating an encounter with the word of God that is simple, insightful, and engaging. A great resource for the New Evangelization."

■ **HOSFFMAN OSPINO**, *Professor, Boston College School of Theology and Ministry*

"I most strongly recommend this series, exceptional for its scholarly solidity, pastoral practicality, and clarity of presentation. The church owes Binz a great debt of gratitude for his generous and competent labor in the service of the word of God."

■ **PETER C. PHAN**, *Professor of Catholic Social Thought, Georgetown University*

"*Threshold Bible Study* is an enriching and enlightening approach to understanding the rich faith which the Scriptures hold for us today. All the elements work together to offer the reader a wonderful insight into how the sacred texts of our faith can touch our lives in a profound and practical way today. I heartily recommend this series to both individuals and to Bible study groups."

■ **ABBOT GREGORY J. POLAN, OSB**, *Conception Abbey,*
Abbot Primate of the Benedictine Order

"Stephen J. Binz is a consistently outstanding Catholic educator and communicator whose books on the study and application of Scripture have thoroughly enriched my Christian understanding. In our fast-moving, often confusing times, his ability to help us examine and comprehend the truth through all the noise is especially needed and valuable."

■ **ELIZABETH SCALIA**, *writer and speaker, Editor at Aleteia, blogger at The Anchoress*

"Stephen Binz has created an essential resource for the new evangelization rooted in the discipleship process that helps participants to unpack the treasures of the Scriptures in an engaging and accessible manner. *Threshold Bible Study* connects faith learning to faithful living, leading one to a deeper relationship with Christ and his body, the church."

■ **JULIANNE STANZ**, *Director of New Evangelization, Diocese of Green Bay*

"*Threshold Bible Study* is a wonderful series that is sure to open new doors for every reader. In a practical, pastoral, and accessible manner, Stephen Binz brings the insights of contemporary scholarship to us in understandable language and clear format, inviting readers to deeper reflection on their own lived experience."

■ **BISHOP KEVIN VANN**, *Bishop of Orange*

SALVATION OFFERED
for ALL PEOPLE

Romans

STEPHEN J. BINZ

TWENTY-THIRD
PUBLICATIONS
twentythirdpublications.com

TWENTY-THIRD PUBLICATIONS
One Montauk Avenue, Suite 200
New London, CT 06320
(860) 437-3012 or (800) 321-0411
www.twentythirdpublications.com

ISBN: 978-1-62785-343-9
Library of Congress Control Number: 2017958808
Printed in the U.S.A.

 A division of Bayard, Inc.

Contents

LESSONS 13–18

LESSONS 19–24

LESSONS 25–30

How to Use
Threshold Bible Study

Threshold Bible Study is a dynamic, informative, inspiring, and life-changing series that helps you learn about Scripture in a whole new way. Each book will help you explore new dimensions of faith and discover deeper insights for your life as a disciple of Jesus.

The threshold is a place of transition. The threshold of God's word invites you to enter that place where God's truth, goodness, and beauty can shine into your life and fill your mind and heart. Through the Holy Spirit, the threshold becomes holy ground, sacred space, and graced time. God can teach you best at the threshold, because God opens your life to his word and fills you with the Spirit of truth.

Threshold Bible Study approaches each topic or book of the Bible in a thematic way. You will understand and reflect on the biblical texts through overarching themes derived from biblical theology. Through this method, the study of Scripture will impact your life in a unique way and transform you from within.

These books are designed for maximum flexibility. Each study is presented in a workbook format, with sections for reading, reflecting, writing, discussing, and praying. Each *Threshold* book contains thirty lessons, which you can use for your daily study over the course of a month or which can be divided into six lessons per week, providing a group study of six weekly sessions. These studies are ideal for Bible study groups, small Christian communities, adult faith formation, student groups, Sunday school, neighborhood groups, and family reading, as well as for individual learning.

The commentary that follows each biblical passage launches your reflection on that passage and helps you begin to see its significance within the context of your contemporary experience. The questions following the commentary challenge you to understand the passage more fully and apply it to your own life. Space for writing after each question is ideal for personal study and also allows group participants to prepare in advance for the weekly discussion. The prayer helps conclude your study each day by integrating your learning into your relationship with God.

The method of *Threshold Bible Study* is rooted in the ancient tradition of *lectio divina*, whereby studying the Bible becomes a means of deeper intimacy with God and a transformed life. Reading and interpreting the text (*lectio*) is followed by reflective meditation on its message (*meditatio*). This reading and reflecting flows into prayer from the heart (*oratio* and *contemplatio*). In this way, one listens to God through the Scripture and then responds to God in prayer.

This ancient method assures you that Bible study is a matter of both the mind and the heart. It is not just an intellectual exercise to learn more and be able to discuss the Bible with others. It is, more importantly, a transforming experience. Reflecting on God's word, guided by the Holy Spirit, illumines the mind with wisdom and stirs the heart with zeal.

Following the personal Bible study, *Threshold Bible Study* offers ways to extend personal *lectio divina* into a weekly conversation with others. This communal experience will allow participants to enhance their appreciation of the message and build up a spiritual community (*collatio*). The end result will be to increase not only individual faith, but also faithful witness in the context of daily life (*operatio*).

When bringing *Threshold Bible Study* to a church community, try to make every effort to include as many people as possible. Many will want to study on their own; others will want to study with family, a group of friends, or a few work associates; some may want to commit themselves to share insights through a weekly conference call, daily text messaging, or an online social network; and others will want to gather weekly in established small groups.

By encouraging *Threshold Bible Study* and respecting the many ways people desire to make Bible study a regular part of their lives, you will widen the number of people in your church community who study the Bible regularly in whatever way they are able in their busy lives. Simply sign up people at the Sunday services and order bulk quantities for your church. Encourage people to follow the daily study as faithfully as they can. This encouragement can be through Sunday announcements, notices in parish publications, support on the church website, and other creative invitations and motivations.

Through the spiritual disciplines of Scripture reading, study, reflection, conversation, and prayer, *Threshold Bible Study* will help you experience God's grace more abundantly and root your life more deeply in Christ. The risen Jesus said: "Listen! I am standing at the door, knocking; if you hear my voice and open the door, I will come in to you and eat with you, and you with me" (Rev 3:20). Listen to the Word of God, open the door, and cross the threshold to an unimaginable dwelling with God!

SUGGESTIONS FOR INDIVIDUAL STUDY

- Make your Bible reading a time of prayer. Ask for God's guidance as you read the Scriptures.

- Try to study daily, or as often as possible according to the circumstances of your life.

- Read the Bible passage carefully, trying to understand both its meaning and its personal application as you read. Some persons find it helpful to read the passage aloud.

- Read the passage in another Bible translation. Each version adds to your understanding of the original text.

- Allow the commentary to help you comprehend and apply the scriptural text. The commentary is only a beginning, not the last word, on the meaning of the passage.

- After reflecting on each question, write out your responses. The very act of writing will help you clarify your thoughts, bring new insights, and amplify your understanding.

- As you reflect on your answers, think about how you can live God's word in the context of your daily life.

- Conclude each daily lesson by reading the prayer and continuing with your own prayer from the heart.

- Make sure your reflections and prayers are matters of both the mind and the heart. A true encounter with God's word is always a transforming experience.

- Choose a word or a phrase from the lesson to carry with you throughout the day as a reminder of your encounter with God's life-changing word.

- Share your learning experience with at least one other person whom you trust for additional insights and affirmation. The ideal way to share learning is in a small group that meets regularly.

SUGGESTIONS FOR GROUP STUDY

- Meet regularly; weekly is ideal. Try to be on time and make attendance a high priority for the sake of the group. The average group meets for about an hour.

- Open each session with a prepared prayer, a song, or a reflection. Find some appropriate way to bring the group from the workaday world into a sacred time of graced sharing.

- If you have not been together before, name tags are very helpful as a group begins to become acquainted with the other group members.

- Spend the first session getting acquainted with one another, reading the Introduction aloud, and discussing the questions that follow.

- Appoint a group facilitator to provide guidance to the discussion. The role of facilitator may rotate among members each week. The facilitator simply keeps the discussion on track; each person shares responsibility for the group. There is no need for the facilitator to be a trained teacher.

- Try to study the six lessons on your own during the week. When you have done your own reflection and written your own answers, you will be better prepared to discuss the six scriptural lessons with the group. If you have not had an opportunity to study the passages during the week, meet with the group anyway to share support and insights.

- Participate in the discussion as much as you are able, offering your thoughts, insights, feelings, and decisions. You learn by sharing with others the fruits of your study.

- Be careful not to dominate the discussion. It is important that everyone in the group be offered an equal opportunity to share the results of their work. Try to link what you say to the comments of others so that the group remains on the topic.

- When discussing your own personal thoughts or feelings, use "I" language. Be as personal and honest as appropriate and be very cautious about giving advice to others.

- Listen attentively to the other members of the group so as to learn from their insights. The words of the Bible affect each person in a different way, so a group provides a wealth of understanding for each member.

- Don't fear silence. Silence in a group is as important as silence in personal study. It allows individuals time to listen to the voice of God's Spirit and the opportunity to form their thoughts before they speak.

- Solicit several responses for each question. The thoughts of different people will build on the answers of others and will lead to deeper insights for all.

- Don't fear controversy. Differences of opinions are a sign of a healthy and honest group. If you cannot resolve an issue, continue on, agreeing to disagree. There is probably some truth in each viewpoint.

- Discuss the questions that seem most important for the group. There is no need to cover all the questions in the group session.

- Realize that some questions about the Bible cannot be resolved, even by experts. Don't get stuck on some issue for which there are no clear answers.

- Whatever is said in the group is said in confidence and should be regarded as such.

- Pray as a group in whatever way feels comfortable. Pray for the members of your group throughout the week.

Schedule for Group Study

SESSION 1: INTRODUCTION DATE: _____

SESSION 2: LESSONS 1–6 DATE: _____

SESSION 3: LESSONS 7–12 DATE: _____

SESSION 4: LESSONS 13–18 DATE: _____

SESSION 5: LESSONS 19–24 DATE: _____

SESSION 6: LESSONS 25–30 DATE: _____

I have written to you rather boldly by way of reminder,
because of the grace given me by God to be a minister of Christ Jesus
to the Gentiles in the priestly service of the gospel of God,
so that the offering of the Gentiles may be acceptable,
sanctified by the Holy Spirit. ROMANS 15:15–16

Salvation Offered to All People

As Paul's longest and most developed writing, his monumental Letter to the Romans stands first in the church's collection of Paul's literary work. It has served to introduce Paul's thought to generations of readers and is recognized as his most influential and controversial work. At the time of the Reformation, the letter became a battleground for a Christianity being pulled apart. Ironically, a work that Paul intended to unify the church of his own day has been used as a wedge causing separation and division. Fortunately, a renewed understanding of Romans has led to ecumenical understanding and a deepening unity among Christians today.

When Paul penned this letter to "all God's beloved in Rome," he was writing to a church that he had neither founded nor as yet visited. Unlike his other letters, in which he wrote to communities who knew him well and addressed pastoral concerns of those churches, in his Letter to the Romans he addressed the Christians of a city he has never seen. Paul wrote in anticipation of his intended visit. He had carried out his task of preaching in the eastern Mediterranean world, and now he was ready to undertake the proclamation of the gospel in the western half of that world. He hoped to make this political, military, and economic capital of the empire the base of his future mission. This letter serves as both his personal introduction to the church in Rome and an exposition of his developed understanding of the gospel.

The church in Rome, like most all the earliest churches of Christianity, was established by Jewish Christians. The synagogues provided the arena for evangelization. But several years before Paul's writing, trouble stirred among the Jews in Rome, and Claudius, the emperor from 41 to 54, expelled the Jewish population from the city (Acts 18:2). The Roman historian Suetonius states that Claudius "expelled Jews who were making constant disturbances at the instigation of Chrestus." Most historians believe that Suetonius misunderstood the Christian title of the Messiah, confusing Christus, the Latin name for Christ, with the more common name, Chrestus. It seems that this conflict between Jews and Jewish Christians over the status of Jesus as Messiah led to their banishment from Rome in the late 40s.

After the expulsion of the Jewish Christian leadership of the church in Rome, the Gentile Christians took the leadership positions and set up a church increasingly less influenced by the synagogue and concern for Jewish identity. This continued until the death of Claudius in 54, when many Jews returned to the capital city. The resulting tension between the Jewish and Gentile Christians seems to have been the occasion of Paul's letter. He wrote to explain his understanding of the equal relationship of Jews and Gentiles within the united People of God. He clarified to Jews that God's plan of salvation intended to include the Gentiles from the beginning, and he taught the Gentiles to respect the essential Jewish heritage of their faith.

Paul meant his letter to be read aloud to the community of believers while assembled at the house churches in Rome, intending that it be heard and understood by practicing Christians in the middle of the first century. For those who listened, Paul demonstrated how Gentiles can be incorporated with Jews into God's people without jeopardizing the continuity of salvation history. He shows that God desires salvation for people of all races and that salvation is offered, not through observing the precepts of the Torah, but by God's grace through the sacrifice of Jesus Christ.

Reflection and Discussion

- What difficulties might Paul have encountered in writing to the Romans due to the fact that he had never personally visited the Christian community there?

- What might be some tensions between the Christian Jews and Gentiles? Why is Paul so concerned to bring unity between them?

Sin, Grace, Law, and Faith

One of the things about which the Jewish and Gentile Christians were in complete agreement was the authority of Scripture—the Torah and the prophets—and its role in presenting God's saving plan. For this reason, Paul expressed his understanding of the gospel by continual references to the Scriptures of Israel and God's unfolding design. The prophets had communicated God's promise of a final liberation, and now, in the gospel of Jesus Christ, God has spoken his final word and brought saving history to its climax.

Paul's foundational premise is that all people are under the domination of sin: "All have sinned and fall short of the glory of God" (3:23). The opening stories of Genesis show that sin has been around for as long as humanity. It is not a part of the Creator's design, but the result of human choice and failure. Sin dominates the human condition and is the cause of separation, alienation, division—from God, from others, and from oneself. It creates a destructive solidarity of sinners, from one generation to the next, making them slaves to the forces that oppose God and hindering them from being bearers of the divine image. As Creator and Lord, God has every right to judge his human creation on the basis of its choices and behaviors, and divine wrath toward a disobedient creation is fully justified.

The only way that human creatures can be delivered from its addiction to sin is through something more powerful. Paul weighs what he says about sin against a power that he calls grace. This is God's merciful favor toward his people, which they have neither earned nor deserve. Grace is manifested in God's call and promises to Abraham, his choice of Israel, and most fully in the salvation of sinful human beings through Jesus Christ. Sin leads to death; grace leads to life. Paul proclaims the good news that "where sin increased, grace abounded all the more, so that, just as sin exercised dominion in death, so grace might also exercise dominion through justification leading to eternal life through Jesus Christ our Lord" (5:20–21).

Paul's exposition of human history divides it into two ages. Prior to Christ, humanity was under the power of sin, represented by the story of Adam's disobedience. All human beings are born into this sinfulness of humanity's Adam-like existence. But through the new birth of baptism, people are joined to Christ and his obedience. Adam and Christ are both archetypes for humanity's direction and possibilities: Adam through sin moves toward death; Christ through God's grace moves toward life. Rather than giving his creatures what they deserve, God looks with mercy on his creature's rebellion and offers them life.

Paul refers to "the law" as that set of regulations intended by God to guide Israel in its covenant with God. This law of Moses, Paul says, is "holy and just and good" (7:12). But this law has proved incapable of overcoming humanity's foundational problem, its slavery to sin. Telling the Jews to just obey the regulations of the Torah has become as futile as telling slaves to simply try harder. In fact, the good and holy law has fallen under the dominance of sin and has become its instrument. The law, then, intensifies the effects of whatever force holds sway over human beings, whether that force be sin or grace. As Paul explains, the law, which was intended to guide God's people, actually provokes people's tendency to resist the will of their Creator and arouses human desires toward sinfulness. In addition, the written law makes explicit the fact that sin is a clear rebellion against God, a transgression of his holy will, and thereby enhances the power of sin.

God desires to bring all people from the slavery of sin to the experience of grace in Jesus Christ. This offer of salvation must be accepted and received—by both Jews and Gentiles—through what Paul calls "faith" (*pistis*, in Greek). The word translated "faith" in most English versions of Scripture has a broad range of meanings. It includes belief, confidence, assurance, faithfulness, commitment, loyalty, and allegiance. For Paul, faith means the free commitment of oneself to God in Jesus Christ, the submission of one's intellect and will to God.

Christian culture today offers lots of prepackaged ideas about the meaning of faith, law, works, and salvation that simplify and distort the full message of the New Testament. Statements like "I am saved because I trust in the blood of Jesus" or "Faith apart from works saves me" do not accurately summarize the gospel. In this letter, Paul leads his readers to a more robust understanding of Christian faith and its implication.

Faith and works are too often pitted against each other as opposite paths to salvation, one that is successful (faith) and one that fails (works). This division depends on partial and inaccurate meanings of faith and works. When Paul says, "we hold that a person is justified by faith apart from works prescribed by the law" (3:28), he is not speaking about good works in general, but works demanded by the law of Moses. He is demonstrating that both Jews and Gentiles are justified on the ground of the same faith.

Jews can no longer expect God's saving grace simply by virtue of their race. Just living the precepts of the covenant cannot unbind a person from the reign of sin. And Gentiles should not be expected to become practicing Jews before they can experience salvation in Christ. No, for Jew and for Gentile, salvation is received by God's grace through the act of faith.

Through a sincere search for Paul's meaning in this letter, we discover that faith and works are not mutually exclusive after all. If salvation is through faith—understood as faithfulness, commitment, and allegiance to Jesus Christ—then the fatiguing discussion about whether we are saved by faith alone or by faith and works would no longer divide. With this understanding of faith, we realize how good works done in love are inseparable from a life lived in Christ. Through our honest study of Romans, perhaps Paul can again bring healing to our fractured Christianity.

Reflection and Discussion

- Why is grace necessary for us to overcome sin?

- What does Paul mean by faith? How does this understanding overcome the divisive conflict between faith and works?

What God Has Done for Humanity in Christ

Paul does not narrate the earthly ministry of Jesus, his preaching or his miracles. Rather, he teaches what God has done for humanity, both Jews and Gentiles, through the life, ministry, death, burial, resurrection, and enthronement of Christ. This work of God on our behalf is God's gift rooted in divine love: "God proves his love for us in that while we were still sinners Christ died for us" (5:8). This act of divine love is humanly inconceivable and contrary to all expectations. It is unconditional and independent of any worthiness or merit on our part. God's climactic and decisive action on behalf of humanity is God's free act of grace.

In describing what God has achieved for humanity in Christ, Paul makes use of several different images, each drawn from his own first-century background. Each image expresses a distinct facet of Christ's climactic work and the effects offered to all people. Here is a brief description of each of these images that will appear throughout Paul's letter:

Justification. This is the primary image Paul uses in Romans, expressing the new relationship between human beings and God because of the work of Christ. Justification is a judicial term designating the effect created on those who stand acquitted or vindicated before a judge's tribunal. In relationship to God, sinners stand justified before God because of the work of Christ. People are able to accept and receive this act of grace from God, not through their observance of the precepts of the Mosaic law, but through their response of faith, through faithfulness to Christ and baptism in him. We can stand before God acquitted because we are justified by grace through faith. As Paul says, we are "now justified by his grace" (3:24), and "he justifies the one who has faith in Jesus" (3:26).

Salvation. This image expresses rescue from harm and deliverance from evil. Throughout the Scriptures, God saved his people from harm and evil that was physical and spiritual, internal and external, personal and communal. In introducing his letter, Paul describes the gospel as "the power of God for salvation to everyone who has faith" (1:16). He teaches that we have been saved through Christ's death and resurrection, yet the full effects of our salvation will be experienced in the future. Salvation is an ongoing process that culminates in a glorious future. Paul urges us to be confident in this process as he shows that justification and salvation are two different facets of what God has done for us: "Much more surely then, now that we have been justified by his blood, will we be saved through him from the wrath of God" (5:9).

Reconciliation. This image designates a change in relationship, from one of hostility and alienation to one of friendship and intimacy. When Paul uses this image, he speaks of God reconciling people to himself through Christ, bringing sinners from estrangement to closeness. This reconciliation puts us on the way to salvation, as Paul says: "For if while we were enemies, we were reconciled to God through the death of his Son, much more surely, having been reconciled, will we be saved by his life" (5:10). This reconciliation unites the world back to God, it recovers a lost wholeness and integrity, and it creates again a right relationship between the Creator and creatures.

Adoption. This process for transferring an enslaved or abandoned child into the family of another became an image for God's relationship with

Israel. An adopted child received the sense of belonging to the family and an inheritance. As Paul applies this image to the lives of believers, he describes adoption as God's gift, uniting us to his Son through the Spirit: "You did not receive a spirit of slavery to fall back into fear, but you have received a spirit of adoption" (8:15). This adoption makes us children of God and enables us to acknowledge our adoption by crying out to God, "Abba! Father!" As children, we become heirs in God's family. With Christ we become joint heirs, inheriting all of God's blessings.

Redemption. Paul drew this image from the practice of emancipation of prisoners and slaves. An Israelite who bought back a kinsman who was held captive or enslaved was known as a redeemer. The prophets and psalms describe God as Israel's Redeemer, who freed his people from the bondage of Egypt and the captivity of Babylon. Paul applies this image to Christ when he speaks of the redemption that is in Christ. He even speaks of redemption in a cosmic sense: "We know that the whole creation has been groaning in labor pains until now; and not only the creation, but we ourselves...groan inwardly while we wait for adoption, the redemption of our bodies" (8:22–23).

Atonement. This imagery from ancient Israel refers to God's pardon of sin through offering sacrifice. Paul understands the cross of Jesus and the shedding of his blood as a sacrifice of atonement. The sacrifice of Christ has achieved for humanity all that the Day of Atonement ritual symbolized each year as it was enacted in Jerusalem's temple (Lev 16). Paul expresses what God has done for all sinful people, using the images of justification, redemption, and atonement: "They are now justified by his grace as a gift, through the redemption that is in Christ Jesus, whom God put forward as a sacrifice of atonement by his blood, effective through faith" (3:24–25).

Sanctification. This image comes from Israel's Torah and prophets, where people and things were often referred to as "holy," that is, set apart from the profane world and marked out for God's service. For Paul, Christ is the means whereby believers are made holy, that is, sanctified or made saints. In Romans he says, "Now that you have been freed from sin and enslaved to God, the advantage you get is sanctification. The end is eternal life" (6:22). Sanctification expresses the separation of Christians from a fully secular life to devote themselves to the service of God.

Glorification. The Scriptures of Israel speak of the perceptible manifestation of God's presence as divine "glory." For Paul, glory expresses the destiny of Christian believers. "We boast," he says, "in our hope of sharing the glory of God" (5:2). Not only will we reflect divine glory, but we will share the glory of God, bearing the full image and likeness of God as our Creator intends. Paul encourages the struggling community in Rome, "I consider that the sufferings of this present time are not worth comparing with the glory about to be revealed to us" (8:18). Being glorified by God is presented as the culminating effect of God's saving work in those who put their faith in Christ Jesus (8:30). We trust God completely to finish the work of our salvation and bring us to the glory he has promised.

With all of these various images, drawn from the background of both Jews and Gentiles, Paul describes what God has done for humanity through Jesus Christ. In a city dominated by the cult of the Roman emperor, God offers new and eternal life to those who place their trust and allegiance in God's Messiah and Lord.

Reflection and Discussion

- Why does Paul use such a variety of images to express what God has done for us in Christ?

- These various images refer to both our present and future existence in Christ? Which do I experience most at present and which do I anticipate most in the future?

Reading Paul's Letter to the Romans

Because Paul was a Jew who formerly persecuted Christians and since he was known throughout the eastern world as the Apostle to the Gentiles, Paul recognized that suspicions about his teachings had undoubtedly reached the city of Rome. He also knew that the tensions within the church there between Jewish and Gentile Christians had resulted in misunderstanding and division. Because of these circumstances and since Paul hoped to soon make his first visit to Rome, Paul wrote this letter in order to introduce himself and to clarify for the Christians of Rome how Jews and Gentiles are equally included in God's saving plan and should be united in faith and worship within the church.

Paul had to explain the gospel in such a way that it would be accepted by Jews and Gentiles alike. For this reason, he establishes his teachings on the Torah and prophets of Israel, showing how the new and final era of salvation history has begun in Christ. He shows how God is faithful to his promises, which was essential for Jewish Christians, but he also affirms the universality of those promises, which was necessary for the Gentiles.

Paul's letter is not an abstract work of theology. It is written in the context of his own intentions and the struggles of the people to whom he wrote. This understanding is a great benefit for the modern reader in interpreting the text. In this light, we will divide the letter into four quarters: Rom 1—4, Rom 5—8, Rom 9—11, and Rom 12—16.

In the opening chapter, Paul introduces himself and his purpose for writing. He praises his audience and makes clear that his focus is "the gospel," to which he has dedicated his life. He describes the gospel as "the power of God for salvation to everyone who has faith" (1:16). Wanting to lead "everyone" to salvation, he intends to explain how all people can belong to Jesus Christ. But he sets this purpose aside for a while because, first, he will demonstrate that all of humanity needs salvation because the reign of sin is universal. Rom 2 spotlights how the Jewish people are accountable to God for sin, and Rom 3 widens the light to detail the guilt of all people. Paul then begins to show the way out, the path of salvation. Human beings cannot be right with God through their own merits, but by squarely facing their sin and appealing to God's grace in the saving work of Jesus Christ. Rom 4 presents the example of Abraham to show that God's promises are realized, not by obedience to the law, but by faithfulness to God.

The next section of the letter contrasts life under the domination of sin, represented by Adam, and life dominated by grace, brought about by Christ. Rom 5 presents the hope of glory that is ours in Christ and the movement toward salvation. Rom 6 describes the victory of grace over the bondage of sin, and Rom 7 describes the triumph of grace over the power of the law. As humanity becomes convinced of its need for a savior, God's grace draws believers into a loyal union with Christ. Paul's climactic words in Rom 8 assure us that we can face all adversity through the love of God manifested in Christ and received through the power of the Holy Spirit.

Paul devotes Rom 9—11 to explaining the relationship of Israel to the gospel. He praises God's promises and faithfulness to Israel, yet acknowledges his perplexity that the gospel has fared worse among Jews than among Gentiles. He then explains how Israel's rejection of the gospel has opened the way for the Gentiles to share in their inheritance. The remnant of Jews who have accepted Jesus as Messiah provides an assurance that, eventually, "all Israel will be saved" (11:26). Finally, Paul assures his listeners that God will demonstrate his mercy to the chosen people because "the gift and the calling of God are irrevocable" (11:29).

The last chapters of Paul's letter present the practical ramifications of the gospel. In Rom 12, Paul urges the Christian community to present their lives as a "living sacrifice to God," using their gifts to benefit one another. Paul pleads for unity in the church, asking his listeners to refrain from judging others, to look to the good of others, and to imitate Christ's acceptance of

Jews and Gentiles. In Rom 15, Paul states his mission to continue establishing churches, his desire to visit Rome, and his request for their prayers. In the final chapter, Paul sends personal greetings to Christians in Rome, whom he calls his "co-workers," and concludes with a prayer of praise to God.

While we must keep in mind Paul's theological, pastoral, and missionary purpose when reading Romans, we must also keep in mind our own context today when reading this work. We are living in an age in which the evil that surrounds us may cause us to lose hope. Paul's letter offers us a confident trust that nothing can separate us from the love of God in Christ Jesus our Lord.

Reflection and Discussion

- What aspects of the church in Rome are important to keep in mind in order to understand Paul's letter?

- What aspects of my own context today make me more open and eager to read this letter?

Prayer

Lord God, you called Paul to be your apostle and to proclaim your gospel to the people of the ancient world. Prepare my mind and heart to receive these inspired words of Paul as I read his Letter to the Romans. Show me how to meditate on these words each day so that they lead me to prayer. Through the work of the Holy Spirit, stir up in me a desire to respond to these words and allow them to transform my life. Keep me faithful these weeks to the challenges of study and prayer that your word offers to me.

SUGGESTIONS FOR FACILITATORS, GROUP SESSION 1

1. If the group is meeting for the first time, or if there are newcomers joining the group, it is helpful to provide name tags.

2. Distribute the books to the members of the group.

3. You may want to ask the participants to introduce themselves and tell the group a bit about themselves.

4. Ask one or more of these introductory questions:
   - What drew you to join this group?
   - What is your biggest fear in beginning this Bible study?
   - How is beginning this study like a "threshold" for you?

5. You may want to pray this prayer as a group:
   Come upon us, Holy Spirit, to enlighten and guide us as we begin this study of Paul's Letter to the Romans. You inspired the authors of Scripture to reveal your presence throughout the history of salvation. This inspired word has the power to convert our hearts and change our lives. Fill our hearts with desire, trust, and confidence as you shine the light of your truth within us. Motivate us to read the Scriptures and give us a deeper love for God's word each day. Bless us during this session and throughout the coming week with the fire of your love.

6. Read the Introduction aloud, pausing at each question for discussion. Group members may wish to write the insights of the group as each question is discussed. Encourage several members of the group to respond to each question.

7. Don't feel compelled to finish the complete Introduction during the session. It is better to allow sufficient time to talk about the questions raised than to rush to the end. Group members may read any remaining sections on their own after the group meeting.

8. Instruct group members to read the first six lessons on their own during the six days before the next group meeting. They should write out their own answers to the questions as preparation for next week's group discussion.

9. Fill in the date for each group meeting under "Schedule for Group Study."

10. Conclude by praying aloud together the prayer at the end of the Introduction.

I am not ashamed of the gospel; it is the power of God for salvation to everyone who has faith, to the Jew first and also to the Greek.
ROMANS 1:16

Paul Addresses God's Beloved in Rome

ROMANS 1:1–17 ¹*Paul, a servant of Jesus Christ, called to be an apostle, set apart for the gospel of God, ²which he promised beforehand through his prophets in the holy scriptures, ³the gospel concerning his Son, who was descended from David according to the flesh ⁴and was declared to be Son of God with power according to the spirit of holiness by resurrection from the dead, Jesus Christ our Lord, ⁵through whom we have received grace and apostleship to bring about the obedience of faith among all the Gentiles for the sake of his name, ⁶including yourselves who are called to belong to Jesus Christ,*

⁷To all God's beloved in Rome, who are called to be saints:

Grace to you and peace from God our Father and the Lord Jesus Christ.

⁸First, I thank my God through Jesus Christ for all of you, because your faith is proclaimed throughout the world. ⁹For God, whom I serve with my spirit by announcing the gospel of his Son, is my witness that without ceasing I remember you always in my prayers, ¹⁰asking that by God's will I may somehow at last succeed in coming to you. ¹¹For I am longing to see you so that I may share with you some spiritual gift to strengthen you—¹²or rather so that we may be mutually encouraged by each other's faith, both yours and mine. ¹³I want you to know, brothers and sisters, that I have often intended to come to you (but thus far have been prevented), in order that I may reap some harvest among you as I have among the rest of the Gentiles. *¹⁴I am a debtor both to Greeks and to barbarians, both to the wise and to the foolish* ¹⁵*—hence my eagerness to proclaim the gospel to you also who are in Rome.*

¹⁶For I am not ashamed of the gospel; it is the power of God for salvation to everyone who has faith, to the Jew first and also to the Greek. ¹⁷For in it the righteousness of God is revealed through faith for faith; as it is written, "The one who is righteous will live by faith."

Paul's introduction of himself to his recipients is considerably expanded in comparison with his other letters (verses 1–6). Because he wants to make a favorable first impression on a community he has never visited, he presents his credentials as an apostle with a worldwide commission to proclaim the gospel of Jesus Christ. Calling himself a "servant," he aligns himself with other servants of the Lord—Moses, Joshua, David, and the prophets—inserting himself into the biblical history of salvation. Calling himself an "apostle," he aligns himself with the Twelve, who were personally called and sent by Christ, and called to be the foundation of his church. Designated both servant and apostle, Paul was "set apart" by God at his conversion to dedicate his life to the "gospel," Paul's one-word summary of God's act of salvation in Christ.

This gospel had been "promised beforehand" by God "through his prophets in the holy scriptures" (verse 2). The good news of Jesus Christ is the goal of Israel's long history as described in the sacred texts of God's people. The prophets have communicated God's promise of a final liberation, and now God has spoken his last word, "the gospel concerning his Son." He was revealed as Son of God in two stages (verses 3–4). According to his human nature, he was born from the royal house of David, the Messiah promised to Israel. According to the Holy Spirit, he was declared as Son of God with power through his resurrection. As descendant of David, Jesus was Son of God in humility and suffering; as Son of God in power, he entered his role as the exalted Lord. In his earthly ministry, he was God's suffering servant; in his heavenly reign, he is the glorious Lord Jesus Christ. From him, Paul has been commissioned to bring about "the obedience of faith" among the Gentiles (verse 5). Paul's description of his calling—producing the obedience of faith—underlines his conviction that faith in the Lord involves commitment and personal engagement, a calling to "belong to Jesus Christ" (verse 6).

Paul praises the Christians in Rome for their faith, testifying that the quality of their faith is an inspiration for the communities scattered across the Greco-Roman world (verse 8). Although Paul can take no credit for their fame, they have been close to his heart, and he has felt a long-standing sense of responsibility for them. For many years, he has drawn them and his desire to visit them into his constant prayer. Paul expresses his reasons for wanting to come to Rome in several purpose statements, which really only present one motive: "to share with you some spiritual gift" (verse 11), "to reap some harvest among you" (verse 13), and "to proclaim the gospel to you" (verse 15). Paul wants to serve Christ through the ministry entrusted to him.

Paul begins to announce the message of his letter by calling his listeners to reflect on the gospel that he proudly proclaims (verse 16). He describes the gospel as "the power of God for salvation," a force that God has unleashed into the world, enabling human beings to experience salvation in a new and decisive way. This salvation is now universal, available to "everyone who has faith." The human response to God's offer of salvation is faith, a committed loyalty to the gospel and allegiance to Jesus the Lord. This universal salvation is offered "to the Jew first and also to the Greek." The Jew is mentioned first so that all people will remember that God's gracious gift belongs to the Jewish heritage. What God revealed in Israel's Messiah was first manifested to the Jewish people, and all other people are invited now to share in it. But in every case, for both Jews and Greeks, salvation is a result of God's grace and accepted through faith.

The gospel reveals the "righteousness of God" (verse 17). This divine attribute is often used to describe God in the Old Testament, designating God's just and saving quality. God manifests this righteousness through his fidelity to the covenant. Saving his people and being faithful to his promises are manifestations of God's righteousness. Paul demonstrates that God's fidelity to the covenant is demonstrated most completely in the saving acts of God's Son—predicted by the prophets, manifested on the cross, and continually made effective in the preaching of the gospel. He emphasizes the centrality of faith for salvation by insisting that God's righteousness is revealed "through faith for faith." In this memorable phrase, Paul intends to say that faith is the means by which a person shares in salvation and that bringing people to faith is the purpose of God's plan. Finally, Paul's quotation from the prophet Habakkuk, "The one who is righteous will live by faith," previews the thought he will develop throughout the letter: the way to justification, salvation, and the fullness of life is through faith—understood as trust, commitment, and loyalty to God in Jesus Christ.

Reflection and Discussion

- What do the words in verse 7 indicate about how God views me?

  God loves me calls me His Beloved!.

- Paul's term "the obedience of faith" shows that in his understanding there is no separation between faith and obedience, believing and doing. How does this deepen my understanding of salvation through faith?

- What are some of the reasons Paul desires to visit Rome? What are some ways I could begin to evangelize in my own environment?

Prayer

Lord Jesus Christ, I pray for the church to which I belong and for the church of Rome today. Since you have led me to belong to you through the power at work in the gospel, continue to strengthen my faith, and help me to be encouraged by the faith of your people.

Ever since the creation of the world his eternal power and divine nature, invisible though they are, have been understood and seen through the things he has made. ROMANS 1:20

Rejecting the Truth About God

ROMANS 1:18–32 ¹⁸*For the wrath of God is revealed from heaven against all ungodliness and wickedness of those who by their wickedness suppress the truth. ¹⁹For what can be known about God is plain to them, because God has shown it to them. ²⁰Ever since the creation of the world his eternal power and divine nature, invisible though they are, have been understood and seen through the things he has made. So they are without excuse; ²¹for though they knew God, they did not honor him as God or give thanks to him, but they became futile in their thinking, and their senseless minds were darkened. ²²Claiming to be wise, they became fools; ²³and they exchanged the glory of the immortal God for images resembling a mortal human being or birds or four-footed animals or reptiles.*

²⁴Therefore God gave them up in the lusts of their hearts to impurity, to the degrading of their bodies among themselves, ²⁵because they exchanged the truth about God for a lie and worshiped and served the creature rather than the Creator, who is blessed forever! Amen.

²⁶For this reason God gave them up to degrading passions. Their women exchanged natural intercourse for unnatural, ²⁷and in the same way also the men, giving up natural intercourse with women, were consumed with passion for one another. Men committed shameless acts with men and received in their own persons the due penalty for their error.

²⁸And since they did not see fit to acknowledge God, God gave them up to a debased mind and to things that should not be done. ²⁹They were filled with every kind of wickedness, evil, covetousness, malice. Full of envy, murder, strife, deceit, craftiness, they are gossips, ³⁰slanderers, God-haters, insolent, haughty, boastful, inventors of evil, rebellious toward parents, ³¹foolish, faithless, heartless, ruthless. ³²They know God's decree, that those who practice such things deserve to die—yet they not only do them but even applaud others who practice them.

Paul establishes a sharp contrast between "the righteousness of God" (verse 17) and "the wrath of God" (verse 18). While it might seem that he has left the good news, note that both divine characteristics are "revealed" by God. Both are elements of the gospel. The energy of God's holiness is manifested both as saving power and as opposition to sin. Later, Paul will speak about "the kindness and the severity of God" (11:22), another way of expressing God's desire to draw us to himself and God's opposition to all that would keep us from experiencing his saving love. The physician who holds a hope for a cure can best reveal to a patient the severity of the diagnosis.

God's wrath is manifested against "ungodliness and wickedness," all of those evils that fracture our relationships with God and others. Ungodliness refers to offenses against God's holiness and love, such as idolatry. Wickedness refers to offenses against human beings, such as injustice. God's wrath is the result of God's holiness and mercy encountering evil motives, choices, and deeds. Although God made humans free to refuse his saving mercy, he did not make us free from the consequences of that refusal. The wrath of God is not like the rage we experience in human relationships, which often involves self-centered vengeance and retaliation. Divine wrath is God's response to the corruption of his good creation. Through the condemnations in the following verses Paul wants to convince human beings that they are lost, but only so that they will accept salvation. Humanity is like the addict who comes to the Twelve Steps. Humanity must come to grips with the hopelessness of its condition before it can trust in a divine power beyond itself to save.

Paul explains that all human beings are capable of knowing God's "eternal power and divine nature" through creation (verse 20). The problem with human sin is not God's hiddenness and therefore humanity's ignorance, but rather God's self-revelation and humanity's rejection of it. Even though the Gentiles are unable to know God as he is revealed through the events of Scripture, God has always revealed his wisdom, power, goodness, and beauty through creation to everyone. So the people of the world are without excuse: "Though they knew God, they did not honor him as God or give thanks to him" (verse 21). Because humanity rejected God, "their senseless minds were darkened."

The problem in human sinfulness, Paul explains, has always been their substitution of what is genuine for what is phony: they exchanged the glory of God for idolatrous images (verse 23), they exchanged the truth about God for a lie (verse 25), and they exchanged what is natural for what is unnatural (verse 26). Sin is a perversion of what was originally true and good.

Paul describes God's wrath not as fire from heaven or an anger-induced calamity, but rather as letting humanity have its own way. After naming the sins of humanity, he says, "God gave them up to" the natural consequences of their choices (verses 24, 26, 28). Each of these sins from Paul's salvo of over twenty "things that should not be done" produces its own due punishment (verses 28–31). And approval of the behavior of others who do these things is as bad as the actual behavior (verse 32). No one is guilty of all of these sins, nor is anyone innocent of them either. A life that demotes God and promotes self leads to eternal death, rather than the merciful salvation God offers humanity through his Son.

Reflection and Discussion

- What are we able to know about God "through the things he has made"? Why does this make all people responsible to honor him and give thanks to him (verses 20–21)?

- In what ways do I worship the things of creation rather than the Creator of all things?

- In what ways is the "wrath" of God different from the angry responses often shown by human beings?

- Describe how one of the sins of verses 29–31 fractures my relationship with God and other people.

Prayer

Good and holy God, the rebellion of humanity is manifested in the way it exchanges your glory for mere idols. Help me to admit my sinfulness and understand the hopelessness of my life apart from the good news of salvation you offer to me.

For it is not the hearers of the law who are righteous in God's sight, but the doers of the law who will be justified. ROMANS 2:13

The Impartiality of God's Judgment

ROMANS 2:1–16 ¹*Therefore you have no excuse, whoever you are, when you judge others; for in passing judgment on another you condemn yourself, because you, the judge, are doing the very same things. ²You say, "We know that God's judgment on those who do such things is in accordance with truth." ³Do you imagine, whoever you are, that when you judge those who do such things and yet do them yourself, you will escape the judgment of God? ⁴Or do you despise the riches of his kindness and forbearance and patience? Do you not realize that God's kindness is meant to lead you to repentance? ⁵But by your hard and impenitent heart you are storing up wrath for yourself on the day of wrath, when God's righteous judgment will be revealed. ⁶For he will repay according to each one's deeds: ⁷to those who by patiently doing good seek for glory and honor and immortality, he will give eternal life; ⁸while for those who are self-seeking and who obey not the truth but wickedness, there will be wrath and fury. ⁹There will be anguish and distress for everyone who does evil, the Jew first and also the Greek, ¹⁰but glory and honor and peace for everyone who does good, the Jew first and also the Greek. ¹¹For God shows no partiality.*

¹²*All who have sinned apart from the law will also perish apart from the law, and all who have sinned under the law will be judged by the law. ¹³For it is not the hearers of the law who are righteous in God's sight, but the doers of the law who will be justified. ¹⁴When Gentiles, who do not possess the law, do instinctively what*

the law requires, these, though not having the law, are a law to themselves. ¹⁵They show that what the law requires is written on their hearts, to which their own conscience also bears witness; and their conflicting thoughts will accuse or perhaps excuse them ¹⁶on the day when, according to my gospel, God, through Jesus Christ, will judge the secret thoughts of all.

Throughout many parts of his letter, Paul uses a literary technique in which he engages in a lively debate with an imaginary opponent. Here Paul envisions a person, "whoever you are," standing in judgment over those whose sins he has described in the previous chapter. Multiple use of the words "judge" and "judgment" in the first three verses indicates the importance of this theme for Paul. He challenges those who would judge another to include themselves in the scope of their accusation. Because God judges "in accordance with truth" and since everyone sins, no one escapes the judgment of God (verses 2–3). Continuing his argument, Paul challenges those who mistake God's kindness, forbearance, and patience as leniency toward sin (verse 4). God does not show compassion in order to excuse sin but to direct sinners to "repentance," to a change of heart accompanied by a reform of life. Those who exploit God's goodness and remain unrepentant are accumulating the wrath that will be revealed on the day of judgment (verse 5).

Although Paul's entire letter emphasizes the incredible mercy of God in Jesus Christ and the importance of faith in him, he makes it clear at the outset that God will judge everyone according to their "deeds" (verse 6). God's final judgment will have two possible outcomes: "eternal life" or "wrath and fury" (verses 7–8). Paul emphasizes these two outcomes are not the result of weighing good deeds and bad deeds on a scale; rather, they are the result of people's persistent lifestyles. Those who patiently do good, consistently seeking those things associated with their eternal destiny—glory, honor, and immortality—will be given what they seek. In contrast, those who live a self-centered life and do evil, not obeying the truth but acting wickedly, will face God's wrath.

As God's promises of salvation have been given to "the Jew first and also the Greek," so also God's judgment is given to "the Jew first and also the

Greek" for those who refuse to follow the truth (verses 9–10). The terms of God's judgment are the same for everyone, "for God shows no partiality" (verse 11). Paul designates the Jews as those who live "under the law" and the Greeks (or Gentiles) as those who live "apart from the law" (verse 12). The law is the whole body of teachings and regulations from Moses contained in Israel's Torah. But as the prophets demonstrate, Israel has failed deplorably to keep the law. Paul emphasizes that the Jews are certainly privileged to have been given this law by God and to be "hearers of the law," but he makes clear that only "the doers of the law" will be justified by God (verse 13).

Jews will not have an advantage over Gentiles at the final judgment because of their possession of the law. Jews will be judged by the law as they follow God's will as they know it from the Torah. Gentiles too will be judged by the way they follow God's will as they know it instinctively. For God's law is "written on their hearts" and "their own conscience" bears witness to it (verses 14–15). So in both sin and salvation, Jews and Gentiles are equal. On the day of judgment, God will not play favorites or hold people to different standards. God will execute true justice because, through the perfect love of Jesus Christ, the hidden desires of all people will be revealed (verse 16).

Reflection and Discussion

- Why does God's patient kindness lead some people to take advantage of it and lead others to repentance (verse 4)?

- How often do I consider that life ultimately offers two paths that end in two destinations? What seems to be the basic distinction between the two ways?

- What is the basis on which our lives will ultimately be judged by God?

- What are the similarities of Paul's teaching in verse 13 to the teaching in the Letter of James 1:22–25?

Prayer

Just and righteous God, you have created all people to share eternal life with you. Open my heart to experience your patient compassion and lead me to repentance. May I live my life in such a way as to inherit the life you have promised me through Jesus Christ.

A person is a Jew who is one inwardly, and real circumcision is a matter of the heart—it is spiritual and not literal. Such a person receives praise not from others but from God. ROMANS 2:29

Seeking a Transformed Heart

ROMANS 2:17–29 ¹⁷*But if you call yourself a Jew and rely on the law and boast of your relation to God* ¹⁸*and know his will and determine what is best because you are instructed in the law,* ¹⁹*and if you are sure that you are a guide to the blind, a light to those who are in darkness,* ²⁰*a corrector of the foolish, a teacher of children, having in the law the embodiment of knowledge and truth,* ²¹*you, then, that teach others, will you not teach yourself? While you preach against stealing, do you steal?* ²²*You that forbid adultery, do you commit adultery? You that abhor idols, do you rob temples?* ²³*You that boast in the law, do you dishonor God by breaking the law?* ²⁴*For, as it is written, "The name of God is blasphemed among the Gentiles because of you."*

²⁵*Circumcision indeed is of value if you obey the law; but if you break the law, your circumcision has become uncircumcision.* ²⁶*So, if those who are uncircumcised keep the requirements of the law, will not their uncircumcision be regarded as circumcision?* ²⁷*Then those who are physically uncircumcised but keep the law will condemn you that have the written code and circumcision but break the law.* ²⁸*For a person is not a Jew who is one outwardly, nor is true circumcision something external and physical.* ²⁹*Rather, a person is a Jew who is one inwardly, and real circumcision is a matter of the heart—it is spiritual and not literal. Such a person receives praise not from others but from God.*

The Jewish people of Paul's day claimed that their covenant with God put them in a position entirely different from that of the Gentiles. They were God's chosen people, had received God's law, and were in a special relationship to God. In this section, Paul takes up the two aspects of Jewish life that, more than any others, pointed to this special status of the Jews: the Torah, through which God teaches them to know his will (verses 17–24), and circumcision, which marks them as the people of the covenant (verses 25–29). While not denying these blessings of God, Paul insists that knowledge of the law and physical circumcision have no value unless they express the interior disposition of their hearts.

Paul then lists four prerogatives that the Jews enjoyed as a result of these blessings of God. A Jew ought to be a guide to the blind, a light to those in darkness, a corrector of the foolish, and a teacher of children (verses 19–20). The blessings that the Jews have received, their uniquely detailed understanding of God's will, renders them responsible to be examples, guides, and mentors for others, with a mission toward the rest of the world. Yet Paul challenges them to examine how they fall short of their responsibilities. Those who teach the moral law to others must hold themselves to the same standards (verses 21–23). Again, Paul teaches that "doing" the law is what matters. Quoting Scripture, Paul reminds the Jews, "The name of God is blasphemed among the Gentiles" because of the contradiction between their claim and their conduct.

Circumcision is the sign of Jewish identity for males. From the time of Abraham, this initiation ritual brought an adherent into the community of Israel. For Jews who follow the Torah, circumcision marks them as members of the covenant. But if a Jew breaks the law, his circumcision becomes, in effect, uncircumcision—not that he ceases to be physically circumcised, but that his standing before God is the same as that of an uncircumcised Gentile (verse 25). The prophets had said similar things centuries before (Jer 9:26). But Paul draws the startling conclusion that this reversal works in the other direction as well. When uncircumcised Gentiles keep the precepts of the law, they are regarded as though they were circumcised (verse 26). In fact, the uncircumcised Gentile who keeps the law convicts the circumcised Jew who does not (verse 27). Paul is recovering Israel's ancient teachings of the "circumcised heart," the interior mark of the covenant that includes internal conversion and moral renewal (Deut 10:16; Jer 4:4). The genuine reality of Judaism and circumcision is not found in the external appearance; "rather, a person is a Jew who is one inwardly, and real circumcision is a matter of the heart" (verse 29). True religion is the external expression of an internal spirituality rooted in the heart.

Reflection and Discussion

- Paul laments the contradiction between the claims and the conduct of his fellow Jews. What similar contradictions would he find within my own Christian community?

- What might be the characteristics of a "circumcised" heart?

- When did my religion become more than an external ritual for me? Who or what helped that to occur?

Prayer

Faithful God, you chose your people to enter a faithful covenant with you, and you guided them in your way through the law. Give me the desire to deepen my relationship with you and to follow the way you have marked for my life.

Now we know that whatever the law says, it speaks to those who are under the law, so that every mouth may be silenced, and the whole world may be held accountable to God. ROMANS 3:19

God's Faithfulness to the Jews

ROMANS 3:1–20 ¹*Then what advantage has the Jew? Or what is the value of circumcision?* ²*Much, in every way. For in the first place the Jews were entrusted with the oracles of God.* ³*What if some were unfaithful? Will their faithlessness nullify the faithfulness of God?* ⁴*By no means! Although everyone is a liar, let God be proved true, as it is written,*

"So that you may be justified in your words,
and prevail in your judging."

⁵*But if our injustice serves to confirm the justice of God, what should we say? That God is unjust to inflict wrath on us? (I speak in a human way.)* ⁶*By no means! For then how could God judge the world?* ⁷*But if through my falsehood God's truthfulness abounds to his glory, why am I still being condemned as a sinner?* ⁸*And why not say (as some people slander us by saying that we say), "Let us do evil so that good may come"? Their condemnation is deserved!*

⁹*What then? Are we any better off? No, not at all; for we have already charged that all, both Jews and Greeks, are under the power of sin,* ¹⁰*as it is written:*

"There is no one who is righteous, not even one;
¹¹*there is no one who has understanding,*
there is no one who seeks God.
¹²*All have turned aside, together they have become worthless;*

> there is no one who shows kindness,
>   there is not even one."
> [13]"Their throats are opened graves;
>   they use their tongues to deceive."
> "The venom of vipers is under their lips."
>   [14]"Their mouths are full of cursing and bitterness."
> [15]"Their feet are swift to shed blood;
>   [16]ruin and misery are in their paths,
> [17]and the way of peace they have not known."
>   [18]"There is no fear of God before their eyes."
> [19]Now we know that whatever the law says, it speaks to those who are under the law, so that every mouth may be silenced, and the whole world may be held accountable to God. [20]For "no human being will be justified in his sight" by deeds prescribed by the law, for through the law comes the knowledge of sin.

In light of Paul's previous discussion describing how Judaism and circumcision make no essential difference when it comes to God's final judgment of humanity, Paul asks the logical follow-up: "What advantage has the Jew?" (verse 1). Paul's Jewish heritage leads him to declare that the benefits are abundant, chiefly because "the Jews were entrusted with the oracles of God" (verse 2). God has spoken to them and, with these words, has established the covenant with them, the essence of which now constitutes the Scriptures of Israel.

By insisting that God's words were "entrusted" to the Jews, Paul shows that divine revelation was not a possession for Israel to store away for itself but a gift that entailed a responsibility to deliver God's message to the rest of creation. By keeping God's revelation to themselves, the Jews have failed in their mission to be a guide to the blind and a light to those in darkness. But, as Israel's history has taught, God remains faithful despite Israel's unfaithfulness (verses 3–4). Even if we must concede that every person is a liar, we must confess that God remains true to his word. Paul confirms this belief with a quotation from Psalm 51:4, which he introduces with the words, "as it is written." The penitential psalm acknowledges a clear contrast between God's people, who acknowledge their sins, and God, who is right in his judging.

The many questions Paul raises in the next verses probably reflect the kinds of queries he encountered during his missionary travels. If God uses human injustice, falsehood, and evil for his own good purposes, then shouldn't we go on sinning to give greater scope to God's work so that more good will come about (verses 5–8)? Paul's response is an emphatic "By no means!" We are each responsible for our own sin. There is a vast difference between God and humanity and between God's judgments and ours. God is perfectly just, true, and good, which enables God to be the only judge of all people.

Although Paul has stated that the Jews have the covenant and the Scriptures, he concludes that all people, "both Jews and Gentiles, are under the power of sin" (verse 9). Paul includes himself and his own people, implying that if God's chosen people cannot make the grade, then no one can. He then draws together a chain of passages from the Scriptures of Israel, showing humanity's utter moral failure and its slavery to sin (verses 10–18). The continual insistence that "there is no one" stresses the universality of the sin that permeates humanity.

Using the imagery of a legal court, Paul insists that "every mouth may be silenced," meaning that the defendants have no more to say in response to the charges brought up against them (verse 19). Everyone in "the whole world" is "held accountable" to the divine Judge, who weighs the evidence and pronounces the verdict. In light of the universality of sin, "no human being will be justified"; that is, no one will be acquitted for following the law (verse 20). For the law brings only a fuller consciousness of sin, but no rescue from it. All people are clearly guilty and await their sentence.

By demonstrating humanity's enslavement to sin, Paul has prepared his audience for the announcement of the gospel. Those familiar with the chain of Scripture verses Paul quotes to expose humanity's sin (verses 10–18) know that each of those verses was surrounded by a fuller context showing God's promise to rescue those who seem helpless in the face of evil. Even when Paul is announcing universal guilt, he does so by hinting that the solution is close at hand. The power of sin requires a power greater than sin to set all people free, a power found only in the gospel of Jesus Christ. To this unexpected good news, Paul now turns.

Reflection and Discussion

- How had the Jews of Paul's day failed in their use of the gifts God had entrusted to them?

- Paul's list of biblical quotations about humanity's thought, speech, and action could be our response to the daily news. What is Paul's purpose in this list of quotes?

- Today humanity judges God, arguing over whether or not God exists, whether he is good, and why God allows this or that to happen. Why would Paul find this reverse judgment preposterous?

Prayer

Hear my prayer, O Lord, in your faithfulness. I have sinned against your holy will in my thoughts, words, and deeds, and in what I have failed to do. Turn my mind to your promises and give me hope in you.

God is one; and he will justify the
circumcised on the ground of faith and the uncircumcised
through that same faith. ROMANS 3:30

Jews and Gentiles Justified by Faith

ROMANS 3:21–31 ²¹*But now, apart from law, the righteousness of God has been disclosed, and is attested by the law and the prophets,* ²²*the righteousness of God through faith in Jesus Christ for all who believe. For there is no distinction,* ²³*since all have sinned and fall short of the glory of God;* ²⁴*they are now justified by his grace as a gift, through the redemption that is in Christ Jesus,* ²⁵*whom God put forward as a sacrifice of atonement by his blood, effective through faith. He did this to show his righteousness, because in his divine forbearance he had passed over the sins previously committed;* ²⁶*it was to prove at the present time that he himself is righteous and that he justifies the one who has faith in Jesus.*

²⁷*Then what becomes of boasting? It is excluded. By what law? By that of works? No, but by the law of faith.* ²⁸*For we hold that a person is justified by faith apart from works prescribed by the law.* ²⁹*Or is God the God of Jews only? Is he not the God of Gentiles also? Yes, of Gentiles also,* ³⁰*since God is one; and he will justify the circumcised on the ground of faith and the uncircumcised through that same faith.* ³¹*Do we then overthrow the law by this faith? By no means! On the contrary, we uphold the law.*

A fter convincing his audience of humanity's slavery to sin, Paul heralds the good news with his sudden "But now!" (verse 21). He turns from the old era of sin's dominion to the new era of salvation. As all stand guilty before the world's Judge, Paul announces, "The righteousness of God has been disclosed." God's righteousness, his fidelity to the covenant, is now being made known to the world through the preaching of the gospel.

Paul describes this new revelation of God's righteousness as both a radical break from the saving history of the past—"apart from law"—and a demonstration of the continuity of God's saving plan—"attested by the law and the prophets." On the one hand, any human effort based on a code of law is woefully insufficient to attain what God has now done for humanity; it cannot be attained by the Jews through following the laws of the Torah or by the Gentiles through following a law of nature. On the other hand, what God is now doing for the world was anticipated in the Scriptures and is in full harmony with everything God has done throughout salvation history. God has not scrapped the covenant or the divine plan to save the world through Israel; rather, God has completed the covenant through Israel's Messiah.

In this new era of the world's history, human beings must receive and take possession of God's saving grace through a relationship of "faith in Jesus Christ" (verse 22). Faith implies an acceptance of what we have received and the acknowledgment of Christ's lordship in our lives. It leads to a commitment to Christ that progressively intensifies. This same response of faith is required of all people, Jew and Gentile alike; "There is no distinction," Paul says, since all people have sinned and are in need of God's grace (verses 22–23). The cross is God's universal answer to humanity's universal need.

Paul uses three of his most important images—justification, redemption, and atonement—to describe the saving grace that God offers to humanity in Christ (verses 24–25). First, sinful human beings are "justified"; that is, God declares the defendants "not guilty," forgiven of all wrongdoing. Second, God offers "redemption," ransoming the captives from the slavery of sin. And third, the cross of Jesus stands as "a sacrifice of atonement by his blood" for the forgiveness of sin.

Since Paul teaches that "a person is justified by faith apart from works prescribed by the law," there is no room for boasting in one's own standing before God (verses 27–28). Although the Jews of Paul's day did not generally believe that they earned salvation through practicing the works of the law, many were indeed confident that their obedience to the law at least marked them out as a member of the covenant. But Paul teaches that faith, or allegiance to Jesus Christ, is the sign that the gospel has transformed the heart of believers and that they belong to the new covenant. When Jews put their faith in the gospel, God will reaffirm them as covenant members on the basis of that faith. And when Gentiles put their faith in the gospel, God will affirm that they have come into the covenant family through that same faith.

In all of this, God shows his faithfulness to humanity and his deep desire to bring rebellious humanity back to himself. Since there is only one God for all people, God will justify all people in the same way—Jew and Gentile, circumcised and uncircumcised (verses 29–30). Doesn't faith in Christ then replace the law of Israel? Paul will show in the following chapters that this is not at all the conclusion he draws. The law has "by no means" been overthrown (verse 31). Rather, the true purpose of the law has been revealed. Through the law, God exposes sin and engenders a proper attitude and behavior toward God's will. The law was never to be God's way of assuring salvation for his people. Rather, it demonstrates the need of a Savior and draws people to put their trust in Christ, fulfilling the intent of the law.

Reflection and Discussion

- What indicates that Paul desires to break down the barriers between Jews and Gentiles?

- Why does Paul use three different images to describe God's saving grace offered in Christ? How does each image deepen my understanding?

- How have I experienced the growth of faith in my life? How do I desire my faith to develop in the future?

- Why is boasting and any kind of self-righteousness excluded from Paul's understanding of God's gift of grace?

Prayer

God of Jews and Gentiles, you are the God of all people, and you desire to bring all to the fullness of life. Since all have sinned and failed to reflect your glory in the world, I place my trust in the grace and salvation you offer in Jesus your Son.

SUGGESTIONS FOR FACILITATORS, GROUP SESSION 2

1. If there are newcomers who were not present for the first group session, introduce them now.

2. You may want to pray this prayer as a group:

   God of all the nations, you have made us to share the fullness of life with you, but we have sinned against your holy will, failed to reflect your glory, and followed mere idols. By experiencing your patient compassion, open our hearts to admit our sinfulness and to follow along the way of repentance. As we study your word given through your apostle Paul, turn our minds to your promises and give us hope in you. Help us to be strengthened by the faith of one another as we place our trust in the grace you offer us in Jesus your Son.

3. Ask one or more of the following questions:
   - What was your biggest challenge in Bible study over this past week?
   - What did you learn about yourself this week?

4. Discuss lessons 1 through 6 together. Assuming that group members have read the Scripture and commentary during the week, there is no need to read it aloud. As you review each lesson, you might want to briefly summarize the Scripture passages of each lesson and ask the group what stands out most clearly from the commentary.

5. Choose one or more of the questions for reflection and discussion from each lesson to talk over as a group. You may want to ask group members which question was most challenging or helpful to them as you review each lesson.

6. Keep the discussion moving, but don't rush the discussion in order to complete more questions. Allow time for the questions that provoke the most discussion.

7. Instruct group members to complete lessons 7 through 12 on their own during the six days before the next group meeting. They should write out their own answers to the questions as preparation for next week's group discussion.

8. Conclude by praying aloud together the prayer at the end of lesson 6, or any other prayer you choose.

He received the sign of circumcision as a seal of the righteousness that he had by faith while he was still uncircumcised. ROMANS 4:11

Abraham as the Model of Faith

ROMANS 4:1–12 ¹*What then are we to say was gained by Abraham, our ancestor according to the flesh?* ²*For if Abraham was justified by works, he has something to boast about, but not before God.* ³*For what does the scripture say? "Abraham believed God, and it was reckoned to him as righteousness."* ⁴*Now to one who works, wages are not reckoned as a gift but as something due.* ⁵*But to one who without works trusts him who justifies the ungodly, such faith is reckoned as righteousness.* ⁶*So also David speaks of the blessedness of those to whom God reckons righteousness apart from works:*

⁷*"Blessed are those whose iniquities are forgiven,*
and whose sins are covered;
⁸*blessed is the one against whom the Lord will not reckon sin."*

⁹*Is this blessedness, then, pronounced only on the circumcised, or also on the uncircumcised? We say, "Faith was reckoned to Abraham as righteousness."* ¹⁰*How then was it reckoned to him? Was it before or after he had been circumcised? It was not after, but before he was circumcised.* ¹¹*He received the sign of circumcision as a seal of the righteousness that he had by faith while he was still uncircumcised. The purpose was to make him the ancestor of all who believe without being circumcised and who thus have righteousness reckoned to them,* ¹²*and likewise the ancestor of the circumcised who are not only circumcised but who also follow the example of the faith that our ancestor Abraham had before he was circumcised.*

Paul invokes Abraham as his exemplar to substantiate his teaching that "a person is justified by faith apart from works prescribed by the law" (3:28). Referring to the life of Abraham as told in Genesis, Paul shows that the patriarch loyally trusted in God's promises of a son and the blessings that would ensue despite overwhelming evidence to the contrary. Despite seemingly insurmountable obstacles—Sarah's barrenness, his own old age, and decades of waiting—Abraham remained faithful to the relationship God established with him.

If anyone had a reason to boast, it would be Abraham (verse 2). He left his homeland at God's command to travel to an unknown territory, and he carved out a life for Sarah and himself as a nomad in Canaan. But God's promises to Abraham were not a reward for Abraham's good performance, for God called Abraham and promised him blessings and progeny before he had responded in obedience (Gen 12:1–3).

Paul quotes the important text from Genesis: "Abraham believed God, and it was reckoned to him as righteousness" (Gen 15:6; Rom 4:3). The word translated "reckoned" comes from bookkeeping vocabulary meaning "credit to one's account." Because of Abraham's loyal faith in God's promises, God graciously credited to his "account" the status of righteousness (being in a right relationship with God).

Paul illustrates his teaching by giving an example from everyday life. While a laborer has a right to wages based upon the work completed, one who has done no work has no right to any benefits (verses 4–5). Anyone in this situation must depend on the favor and mercy of the other. In the presence of God, all people are in this situation. God, "who justifies the ungodly," justifies people by faith, and that faith is "reckoned as righteousness" by God.

Quoting the opening lines of Psalm 32, one of the Psalms of David, Paul emphasizes God's graciousness. Like Abraham, any number of laudable things could be said of David. But his works were insufficient to make up for his sins. His "blessedness" is due to the forgiveness of his sins, an act of God's grace. Blessed are all those to whom "God reckons righteousness apart from works" of the law (verses 6–8).

Paul's Jewish contemporaries believed that God justifies those within the covenant of Israel, while the ungodly Gentiles stand outside the covenant. But Paul challenges that assumption by arguing that "faith was reckoned to Abraham as righteousness" before he was circumcised (verses 9–10). Abraham was justified through his faithfulness to God and the promises of God. Only later did he received the sign of circumcision as a confirmation or "seal of the righteousness that he had by faith while he was still uncircumcised" (verse 11).

Abraham was an uncircumcised Gentile when he was justified by God. Thus, Abraham was the father of Gentile believers before he was the father of Jewish believers. For Paul and the early Christian church, this meant that both Gentile and Jewish followers of Jesus could appeal to Abraham as father. Abraham is the "ancestor of all who believe" (verse 11). Both groups are included within Abraham's fatherhood of faith, and neither is pitted against the other. Through Abraham we know that trusting faith in God is not a new means for entering the covenant with God, but rather the oldest and truest means. We become descendants of Abraham by following his faith, not his bloodline.

Reflection and Discussion

- How does the example of Abraham demonstrate that justification (righteousness) is a matter of grace on God's side and a matter of faith on the human side?

- What does the life of Abraham teach me about the meaning of faith in Christ?

- In what sense is Abraham called "the ancestor of all who believe"?

- Does it matter to me whether a right relationship with God is a gift to be received or a reward to be earned? What difference does it make to me practically and emotionally?

Prayer

God of our ancestors, you extended to the whole world the blessings you promised to Abraham. Help me realize that I cannot earn your salvation but can only gratefully accept the gift of your salvation through a living faith in Jesus Christ.

Hoping against hope, he believed that he would become "the father of many nations," according to what was said, "So numerous shall your descendants be." ROMANS 4:18

Abraham the Father of Many Nations

ROMANS 4:13–25 ¹³*For the promise that he would inherit the world did not come to Abraham or to his descendants through the law but through the righteousness of faith.* ¹⁴*If it is the adherents of the law who are to be the heirs, faith is null and the promise is void.* ¹⁵*For the law brings wrath; but where there is no law, neither is there violation.*

¹⁶*For this reason it depends on faith, in order that the promise may rest on grace and be guaranteed to all his descendants, not only to the adherents of the law but also to those who share the faith of Abraham (for he is the father of all of us,* ¹⁷*as it is written, "I have made you the father of many nations")* —*in the presence of the God in whom he believed, who gives life to the dead and calls into existence the things that do not exist.* ¹⁸*Hoping against hope, he believed that he would become "the father of many nations," according to what was said, "So numerous shall your descendants be."* ¹⁹*He did not weaken in faith when he considered his own body, which was already as good as dead (for he was about a hundred years old), or when he considered the barrenness of Sarah's womb.* ²⁰*No distrust made him waver concerning the promise of God, but he grew strong in his faith as he gave glory to God,* ²¹*being fully convinced that God was able to do what he had promised.* ²²*Therefore his faith "was reckoned to him as righteousness."* ²³*Now the words, "it was reckoned to him," were written not for his sake alone,* ²⁴*but for ours also. It will be reckoned to*

us who believe in him who raised Jesus our Lord from the dead, ²⁵*who was handed over to death for our trespasses and was raised for our justification.*

This passage continues Paul's exposition of God's intention in establishing the covenant with Abraham, and hence the nature of Abraham's family. The promises, given to Abraham nearly two millennia before Paul, would not remain the possession of only one segment of humanity. Like yeast in the dough, Abraham's descendants would grow to permeate the whole world. His offspring would surpass the bounds of Israel and include the Gentiles so that God's salvation would be offered to everyone. Abraham is the "father of many nations"; he is the "father of us all" (verses 16–18).

The God in whom Abraham believed is the God "who gives life to the dead and calls into existence the things that do not exist" (verse 17). Abraham experienced these manifestations of the God of life. The bodies of Abraham and Sarah were dead to the possibility of producing an heir, but God brought life to them. At the moment when their beloved son was doomed to die in sacrifice, God held back the knife and restored their son to life. The creating and redeeming God of Abraham brought an inheritance into being in a way that seemed totally impossible.

The only response to such a God is faith. Trying to earn the favor of such a God or merit his blessings would be foolish. But faith in the God of the impossible brings hope for the future. God transformed the obstacles Abraham encountered into possibilities for something beyond his dreams. Abraham's faith was not an easy choice; it was a constant struggle. He questioned God, doubted God, pleaded with God. And through this struggle his faith became stronger. For Abraham, his unyielding response was always faithful trust in God's promises (verses 20–21).

This same God of the impossible was also Paul's God. And Paul seeks to persuade us through his writing that this same creating and redeeming God is our God too. The God of Abraham is the God "who raised Jesus our Lord from the dead" (verse 24). The faith of Abraham is a model for all believers—Jews and Gentiles. It is the same faith in the same God who brings the dead to life.

Abraham is the key to understanding the meaning of God's grace and the human response in faith. God met Abraham and brought him into covenant from the same starting point as all Gentiles. God's call and promise to Abraham were independent of Abraham's merit or achievement. But that is not where God left him. Abraham's initial trust in God's promises was just the beginning of a long process of God's leading, testing, and transforming Abraham. Justification by grace through faith, creation from nothing, and resurrection from the dead are all affirmations of the same reality. They bear witness to the power of God to evoke new life in circumstances that seem impossible, in situations in which our only response can be grateful and persistent fidelity.

Reflection and Discussion

• How is God revealed in Abraham's life as the one "who gives life to the dead and calls into existence the things that do not exist"?

• What does justification through faith, creation from nothing, and resurrection from the dead tell me about the nature of God? How has God worked within me to bring faith out of doubt, hope out of impossibility, life out of death?

Prayer

Creating and redeeming God, you create out of nothing and raise the dead to life. Thank you for offering me the grace of salvation, not through my own merits but through Christ, "who was handed over to death for our trespasses and was raised for our justification."

Suffering produces endurance, and endurance produces character, and character produces hope, and hope does not disappoint us, because God's love has been poured into our hearts through the Holy Spirit. ROMANS 5:3–5

Transformed by the Love of God

ROMANS 5:1–11 ¹*Therefore, since we are justified by faith, we have peace with God through our Lord Jesus Christ, ²through whom we have obtained access to this grace in which we stand; and we boast in our hope of sharing the glory of God. ³And not only that, but we also boast in our sufferings, knowing that suffering produces endurance, ⁴and endurance produces character, and character produces hope, ⁵and hope does not disappoint us, because God's love has been poured into our hearts through the Holy Spirit that has been given to us.*

⁶*For while we were still weak, at the right time Christ died for the ungodly. ⁷Indeed, rarely will anyone die for a righteous person—though perhaps for a good person someone might actually dare to die. ⁸But God proves his love for us in that while we still were sinners Christ died for us. ⁹Much more surely then, now that we have been justified by his blood, will we be saved through him from the wrath of God. ¹⁰For if while we were enemies, we were reconciled to God through the death of his Son, much more surely, having been reconciled, will we be saved by his life. ¹¹But more than that, we even boast in God through our Lord Jesus Christ, through whom we have now received reconciliation.*

s a result of our being "justified by faith," we are in a state of grace, experiencing peace with God, surrounded by God's loving generosity (verses 1–2). We realize that this is what we were made for, what human existence ought to be like. We can look to the future with confidence, even "boasting"—a term Paul previously excluded from the Christian life (3:27). But instead of describing a prideful self-confidence, resting on one's own achievement or privileged status, Paul now proposes a boasting that is certainly legitimate because it rests solely on the work God has done on our behalf.

When we accept the grace of Christ's redeeming death through our response in faith, we are "justified" (verse 1) and "reconciled" to God (verse 10). Both words refer to the restoration of our relationship with God that had been lost through the sin of idolatry and injustice. This confident relationship with God in Jesus Christ gives us "peace" and "hope." Peace is the foretaste of the fullness of salvation that we await. Hope is the confident expectation that we will share fully in the glory of God.

God's grace within us is strong enough to give us peace and hope even in the midst of adversity (verses 3–4). Paul knows from his own experience that God's grace enables our sufferings to deepen our hope and lead us to God. Of course, suffering does not necessarily produce "endurance," and endurance doesn't always result in "character." Adversity often produces resentment and bitterness. But endurance, character, and hope are qualities of grace, and they develop when the believer stands justified before God and responds to adversity in faith.

The whole process of God's action on our behalf is rooted in God's love for us. In a way unparalleled by human love, God has given himself to us without restraint: "God's love has been poured into our hearts" (verse 5). This image is that of life-giving water being poured on a thirsty land, torrential rains in an arid desert. God's love gushes forth into our hearts with abandon by the Holy Spirit.

It is impossible for us to understand the dimensions of divine love. But we can see the manifestation of God's love in the death of his Son for us: "God proves his love for us in that while we still were sinners Christ died for us" (verse 8). God's love (*agape* in Greek) is unconditional love, independent of any worthiness or merit on our part. God's act of love is humanly inconceivable and contrary to all expectations (verse 7), demonstrating beyond doubt God's personal love for us, a love that is embodied in the cross of Jesus Christ.

Paul's encouraging text is oriented toward the future when we will be "saved" through Christ (verses 9–10). The peace and hope we experience in the present is just a taste of the fullness of salvation yet to come. We know in our hearts through hope that we will experience the salvation that has been promised us by God. The process of salvation will be complete when we share "the glory of God" (verse 2), the full image and likeness of God, as our Creator intends. In faith we trust God completely to finish the work of our salvation and bring us to the glory he has promised.

Reflection and Discussion

- How does a life move from suffering to endurance, character, and hope (verses 3–4)?

- How does God "prove" his love for us (verse 8)? Why is this proof so convincing?

Prayer

Glorious God, you have given us access to your grace, and I am in awe of the power of your truth and the depths of your love. Open my heart so that your Spirit may fill it with confidence in the glory to come.

**If the many died through the one man's trespass,
much more surely have the grace of God and the free gift in the
grace of the one man, Jesus Christ, abounded for the many.**
ROMANS 5:15

Our Increasing Sin and God's Abundant Grace

ROMANS 5:12–21 [12]*Therefore, just as sin came into the world through one man, and death came through sin, and so death spread to all because all have sinned—* [13]*sin was indeed in the world before the law, but sin is not reckoned when there is no law.* [14]*Yet death exercised dominion from Adam to Moses, even over those whose sins were not like the transgression of Adam, who is a type of the one who was to come.*

[15]*But the free gift is not like the trespass. For if the many died through the one man's trespass, much more surely have the grace of God and the free gift in the grace of the one man, Jesus Christ, abounded for the many.* [16]*And the free gift is not like the effect of the one man's sin. For the judgment following one trespass brought condemnation, but the free gift following many trespasses brings justification.* [17]*If, because of the one man's trespass, death exercised dominion through that one, much more surely will those who receive the abundance of grace and the free gift of righteousness exercise dominion in life through the one man, Jesus Christ.*

[18]*Therefore just as one man's trespass led to condemnation for all, so one man's act of righteousness leads to justification and life for all.* [19]*For just as by the one man's disobedience the many were made sinners, so by the one man's obedience the many will be made righteous.* [20]*But law came in, with the result that the trespass*

multiplied; but where sin increased, grace abounded all the more, ²¹so that, just as sin exercised dominion in death, so grace might also exercise dominion through justification leading to eternal life through Jesus Christ our Lord.

The account of Adam's sin in Genesis is the story of every sinful act. All humanity disputes God's word and rejects God's authority through disobedience. For Paul, therefore, Adam and Christ are both archetypes for humanity's direction and possibilities: Adam represents human existence under the domination of sin; Christ represents humanity dominated by grace. Paul presents these two epochs, signified by Adam and Christ, in sharp contrast. Life in Adam moves toward death; life in Christ moves toward life.

Adam is a corporate figure whose sin expresses the sin of all people. Even though the law that God gave through Moses has served to sharply define sin and hold people accountable for it, sin and its awful consequences have been in the world since humanity's beginnings (verse 13). Thus, Adam is a "type" of Christ, "the one who was to come," in that the universality of sin and death represented by Adam prefigures the universal impact of Christ (verse 14).

Paul then insists that the "free gift" of God's grace in Christ and the "trespass" represented by Adam are not simply balanced as equal and opposite (verse 15). The life–giving benefits that Christ brought to the world far outweigh the mortality and misery brought by sin. The condemnation that has come upon humanity is the direct result of sin, but God has looked on his creatures' rebellion with astounding generosity and given them abundant grace through Christ (verses 16–17). Paul reminds us that we have a choice: the way of Adamic humanity, the way of the past and the way of death; or the way of Christic humanity, the way of the future and the way of life. The choice is ours, but the effects of Christ's saving work have already overcome the effects of Adam's trespass. The grace and righteousness of Christ have defeated the curse and death brought by Adam's sin.

The "act of righteousness" and the "obedience" of Jesus describe what Jesus did throughout his whole life, culminating in his redeeming death as the climax of God's saving plan (verses 18–19). The actions of Jesus embody both the faithfulness of God to the covenant promises and the obedience to the covenant that Israel should have offered to God but failed to do. God's covenant with Israel was intended to be the means of dealing with the sin that had infected the world. Now, in the Messiah, God has realized that purpose and offered justification and life for all, Jews and Gentiles alike.

When God gave the law of Moses as his gift to Israel, trespasses multiplied and sin increased (verse 20). The law was ineffective in dealing with the contagion of sin and revealed more clearly the desperate situation of people apart from grace. But God's grace is more than sufficient to overcome the increase in the power of sin brought by the law. Time after time, the prophets reminded Israel of its sin yet proclaimed God's willingness to show mercy and forgive. Then, in Christ, God's relentless promise to bless all the nations through Israel is definitively fulfilled: "Where sin increased, grace abounded all the more." Although all people are part of Adamic humanity through the solidarity of sinning and thus deserve condemnation, we undeservedly enter Christic humanity with its justification and life through the superabundant grace of God.

Reflection and Discussion

- What are the differences between Adamic humanity and Christic humanity in terms of direction and possibilities?

- What are some of the ways that Paul demonstrates that "where sin increased, grace abounded all the more"?

Ezekel 28.
lucifer

- Why is the law of Moses both inadequate and ineffective in dealing with the power of sin?

- How is God's superabundant grace evident today in the church and in my own life?

Prayer
Just and faithful God, who offers us abundant grace to overcome our trespasses, open my heart to respond in trusting fidelity to your gracious gift of salvation. Make me more aware of my share in sinful humanity and more grateful for your saving grace.

We know that our old self was crucified with him so that the body of sin might be destroyed, and we might no longer be enslaved to sin.

ROMANS 6:6

Dying and Rising with Christ in Baptism

ROMANS 6:1–14 ¹*What then are we to say? Should we continue in sin in order that grace may abound? ²By no means! How can we who died to sin go on living in it? ³Do you not know that all of us who have been baptized into Christ Jesus were baptized into his death? ⁴Therefore we have been buried with him by baptism into death, so that, just as Christ was raised from the dead by the glory of the Father, so we too might walk in newness of life.*

⁵*For if we have been united with him in a death like his, we will certainly be united with him in a resurrection like his. ⁶We know that our old self was crucified with him so that the body of sin might be destroyed, and we might no longer be enslaved to sin. ⁷For whoever has died is freed from sin. ⁸But if we have died with Christ, we believe that we will also live with him. ⁹We know that Christ, being raised from the dead, will never die again; death no longer has dominion over him. ¹⁰The death he died, he died to sin, once for all; but the life he lives, he lives to God. ¹¹So you also must consider yourselves dead to sin and alive to God in Christ Jesus.*

¹²*Therefore, do not let sin exercise dominion in your mortal bodies, to make you obey their passions. ¹³No longer present your members to sin as instruments of wickedness, but present yourselves to God as those who have been brought from death to life, and present your members to God as instruments of righteousness. ¹⁴For sin will have no dominion over you, since you are not under law but under grace.*

Paul's teaching about God's free grace must have prompted many Christians to object. If God's grace is abundant even in the midst of sin, people will assume they can continue doing whatever they wish (verse 1). But Paul's emphatic response to this objection underlines the real death to sin that we experience in Christ and the new life that is ours through faith and baptism (verse 2). If we are united to Christ, then we must bring our lives in line with our new identity.

Paul assumes that the Christians of Rome have a general understanding of baptism, the sacramental action that joins a believer to Christ. Through the tradition they received from the earliest disciples, they know that when a person is "baptized into Christ Jesus" a real change occurs and a new life begins. The believer is transferred from Adamic humanity and begins a step-by-step movement into Christlikeness, participating ever more deeply in the dying and rising of Christ.

The death that the believer undergoes in baptism is a real dying with Christ. Paul says that we are "baptized into his death" (verse 3). This includes our entry into Christ's tomb: "buried with him by baptism into death" (verse 4). Since Christ defeated sin by dying on the cross, in our dying with Christ the power of sin no longer controls our lives. "Our old self was crucified" with Christ; therefore, the dominating influence of sin has been destroyed and we are no longer enslaved to it (verse 6).

But that is only half of Christian baptism. In dying, Christ conquered sin; in rising, he conquered death. As Christ was raised from the dead, we too have the vitality of eternal life within us, so "we too might walk in newness of life" (verse 4). This living in life's newness flows from the resurrection of Jesus. His resurrection was the anticipation of the general resurrection for all. So our life in Christ is a reality that begins in the present as a prelude of our future resurrection. By living in union with Christ, we walk in the age to come.

As Paul turns from theological explanation to moral application, he urges his audience, "Consider yourselves dead to sin and alive to God in Christ Jesus" (verse 11). Our faith and baptism have joined us to the death and life of the Lord, and now it remains for us to seize and claim what Christ has done for us. Freed from sin's enslaving dominion over us, we can now present our lives before another master (verses 12–14). No longer must we offer our bodies to the tyranny of sin as "instruments of wickedness." We can now offer our bodies, with all their members, talents, and abilities, to the reign of God as "instruments of righteousness."

Our life in Christ today is an existence with one foot in the old life and one in the new. We live in the tension between sin and grace, flesh and spirit, death and life. Our fallen human nature pulls in one direction, while our reborn life in Christ pulls even more powerfully in the other. We are already living in the risen Christ, and our freedom from sin and death is evident in the orientation of our lives. Yet, the complete realization of our resurrection awaits the future, when the whole significance of Christ's dying and rising and of our baptism into him will become fully manifest.

Reflection and Discussion

- What aspect of my baptism have I forgotten or neglected? What is Paul teaching me anew in this passage?

- What indicates to me that I am walking today in newness of life, living my future resurrection already in the present?

Prayer

Crucified and risen Lord, in whom I am united through baptism, renew the grace of baptism within me so that sin has no more power in my life. Give me hope in you that I may walk in newness of life.

Thanks be to God that you, having once been slaves of sin, have become obedient from the heart to the form of teaching to which you were entrusted. ROMANS 6:17

The Slavery that Liberates

ROMANS 6:15–23 ¹⁵*What then? Should we sin because we are not under law but under grace? By no means!* ¹⁶*Do you not know that if you present yourselves to anyone as obedient slaves, you are slaves of the one whom you obey, either of sin, which leads to death, or of obedience, which leads to righteousness?* ¹⁷*But thanks be to God that you, having once been slaves of sin, have become obedient from the heart to the form of teaching to which you were entrusted,* ¹⁸*and that you, having been set free from sin, have become slaves of righteousness.* ¹⁹*I am speaking in human terms because of your natural limitations. For just as you once presented your members as slaves to impurity and to greater and greater iniquity, so now present your members as slaves to righteousness for sanctification.*

²⁰*When you were slaves of sin, you were free in regard to righteousness.* ²¹*So what advantage did you then get from the things of which you now are ashamed? The end of those things is death.* ²²*But now that you have been freed from sin and enslaved to God, the advantage you get is sanctification. The end is eternal life.* ²³*For the wages of sin is death, but the free gift of God is eternal life in Christ Jesus our Lord.*

I n response to the objection that freedom from the law frees one to commit sin (verse 15), Paul compares for his listeners two kinds of slavery: the former slavery to sin and a new kind of captivity—the "slavery" that liberates. Both kinds of slavery involve obedience to a master, and Christians are now under obligation to obey their new master. In their former state, they were obedient to sin; in their new life in Christ, they are now "slaves of righteousness" (verse 18) and must take seriously their obedience to God's covenant plan for their salvation.

There is no such thing as human autonomy, a self-sufficiency free from all outside authorities. Either people are under the rule of sin, or they are under the rule of God (verse 16). So the question is not whether one will have a master, but which master one will serve. The former obedience to sin leads ultimately to "death," to final and eternal exclusion from God's presence. But the new obedience, a willing and joyful obedience "from the heart" (verse 17), leads to "righteousness," an acquittal at God's judgment that leads to eternal life.

The change of masters entails a change of heart. Christians are people who have been transformed from within. They possess a willing desire to follow "the form of teaching" to which they have been entrusted. These teachings of the early Christian community include basic creedal beliefs and moral behaviors, which Paul specifies in his other letters. The inner transformation of Christians makes them desire to live in continuity with this community to which they now belong and to be molded by its teachings. Being bound to God and to God's will enables people to become free to be what God desires them to be. Rather than pursuing power, pleasure, and possessions, the enslaving desires of the world, Christians are devoted to "sanctification," the process of becoming holy (verse 19). This new, liberating slavery results in lives that are increasingly God-centered and world-renouncing.

In concluding these thoughts, Paul summarizes the transition from sin to salvation. By asking "what advantage" they gained from the old life of pursuing sin, he convinces sinners that what they thought was true freedom was simply illusory (verses 20–21). But now, "freed from sin and enslaved to God," they gain the advantage of "sanctification" with its final outcome in "eternal life" (verse 22). In his final contrast, Paul describes the penalty that sin exacts as "wages," whereas the result of life in Christ is God's "free gift" (verse 23). Sin earns and merits death, but eternal life is only grace.

Reflection and Discussion

- Why are people never fully autonomous? Why does Paul state that people must serve a master, whether it be sin or God?

- What is the difference in the human heart between obedience to sin and obedience to God?

- How have I experienced the "enslavement" of God that results in "sanctification"?

Prayer

Jesus Christ our Lord, who calls us to the obedience that liberates, give me the desire to turn from the way of sin and to follow in the way that leads to life. Make me holy through your grace so that I may experience even now the free gift of eternal life.

SUGGESTIONS FOR FACILITATORS, GROUP SESSION 3

1. Welcome group members and ask if there are any announcements anyone would like to make.

2. You may want to pray this prayer as a group:

   Just and faithful God, we give you praise for the blessings of salvation and the gift of new life. Make us more aware of our share in sinful humanity and more grateful for your saving grace. Renew within us the grace of baptism so that sin has no more power over us, and give us the gift of a living faith in Jesus Christ. Awed by the power of your truth and the depths of your love, open our hearts so that your Spirit may fill us with confident hope in the glory to come.

3. Ask one or more of the following questions:
   - Which thought from the lessons this week stands out most memorably to you?
   - What is the most important lesson you learned through your study this week?

4. Discuss lessons 7 through 12. Choose one or more of the questions for reflection and discussion from each lesson to discuss as a group. You may want to ask group members which question was most challenging or helpful to them as you review each lesson.

5. Remember that there are no definitive answers for these discussion questions. The insights of group members will add to the understanding of all. None of these questions require an expert.

6. After talking about each lesson, instruct group members to complete lessons 13 through 18 on their own during the six days before the next group meeting. They should write out their own answers to the questions as preparation for next week's group discussion.

7. Ask the group if anyone is having any particular problems with the Bible study during the week. You may want to share advice and encouragement within the group.

8. Conclude by praying aloud together the prayer at the end of one of the lessons discussed. You may add to the prayer based on the sharing that has occurred in the group.

You have died to the law through the body of Christ, so that you may belong to another, to him who has been raised from the dead in order that we may bear fruit for God. ROMANS 7:4

Freedom from Bondage to the Law

ROMANS 7:1–13 ¹*Do you not know, brothers and sisters—for I am speaking to those who know the law—that the law is binding on a person only during that person's lifetime?* ²*Thus a married woman is bound by the law to her husband as long as he lives; but if her husband dies, she is discharged from the law concerning the husband.* ³*Accordingly, she will be called an adulteress if she lives with another man while her husband is alive. But if her husband dies, she is free from that law, and if she marries another man, she is not an adulteress.*

⁴*In the same way, my friends, you have died to the law through the body of Christ, so that you may belong to another, to him who has been raised from the dead in order that we may bear fruit for God.* ⁵*While we were living in the flesh, our sinful passions, aroused by the law, were at work in our members to bear fruit for death.* ⁶*But now we are discharged from the law, dead to that which held us captive, so that we are slaves not under the old written code but in the new life of the Spirit.*

⁷*What then should we say? That the law is sin? By no means! Yet, if it had not been for the law, I would not have known sin. I would not have known what it is to covet if the law had not said, "You shall not covet."* ⁸*But sin, seizing an opportunity in the commandment, produced in me all kinds of covetousness. Apart from*

the law sin lies dead. ⁹I was once alive apart from the law, but when the command-ment came, sin revived ¹⁰and I died, and the very commandment that promised life proved to be death to me. ¹¹For sin, seizing an opportunity in the commandment, deceived me and through it killed me. ¹²So the law is holy, and the commandment is holy and just and good.

¹³Did what is good, then, bring death to me? By no means! It was sin, working death in me through what is good, in order that sin might be shown to be sin, and through the commandment might become sinful beyond measure.

Paul now turns to his teaching on the role of the law, the Torah of Israel, in the life of a Christian. The law of Moses is the whole system of reg-ulations in which the people of Israel were called by God to order their lives under the covenant formed at Mount Sinai. Although the law is "holy and just and good" (verse 12) because it was given by God and reveals God's will, it is limited and provisional. Because its purpose was to lead God's people to Christ, it no longer serves as the definitive expression of God's will for human life. It continues to be a regulating norm for behavior, but it is powerless to produce the obedience and holiness that it demands. Thus, the law reveals our transgressions, makes us more aware of sin, and points to our need of a Savior. Now, as Paul said in the previous chapter, in Christ "you are not under law but under grace" (6:14).

Christians are no longer under the law because our death with Christ in baptism has transferred us from the age of Adam to the new age of Christ. Paul offers the analogy of a woman married to her husband (verses 2–3). Under the law, she had definite restrictions and obligations while married. But if the husband dies, she is released from the marital regulations and is free to marry another. Likewise, we who have experienced death to our old life in Adam are now united with the living Christ and belong to him (verse 4). We now belong to the age of salvation, freed from the dictates of the law so as to live under the lordship of the risen Christ. This spousal union of Christ and the Christian produces the "fruit" of a life dedicated to God.

Paul contrasts life "under the old written code" with "the new life of the Spirit" (verse 6). As a legal code, the law offered a curse on all those who did not observe what it prescribed. As Deuteronomy says, "Cursed be anyone who does not uphold the words of this law by observing them" (Deut 27:26). Such a curse meant "death." But, no longer bound to the old Adam and cut loose from the binding authority of the law, a Christian is freed from its condemning power and energized by God's Spirit.

This does not mean, however, that the one living in Christ has nothing more to do with the law of Moses. The law continues to teach the believer much that is essential about God's holiness and the holiness God expects of his people. In this passage, Paul demonstrates how the powers of sin seized the opportunity of the law and used it for sin's own purposes. Sin has made an ally of what should have been its mortal enemy. In this way, Paul exonerates the law from blame while, at the same time, demonstrating the inability of the law to rescue humanity from its bondage to sin.

Paul speaks in the dramatic first-person "I," identifying himself with the experience of humanity in its struggle with sin. Emphatically stating his belief that the law is good and sin is evil, he demonstrates how sin uses the law. Using the commandment "You shall not covet" as an example, he says that sin exploited the law to stir up within us every sort of covetousness, the desire for everything we do not have (verses 7–8).

Before Moses gave the law to Israel, sin was lifeless, as humanity lived in ignorance of the real nature of its evil conduct. But with the law, sin revived (verse 9). Sin seized the opportunity in the holy commandment and turned it against us. Because of the power of sin, "the very commandment that promised life proved to be death to me" (verse 10). Sin deceives us and spoils the law's life-giving purpose (verse 11). The law is not the culprit; sin is the great offender (verse 13). It abuses the law, producing the opposite of what the law intended. With the coming of the law, sin became understood as a revolt against God, showing humanity in open rebellion against God's will. However much the law of Moses promised life, the power of sin meant that all it could deliver was the deadly curse of disobedience.

Reflection and Discussion

- In what ways does this passage teach me never to underestimate the power of sin? *No Control !*

- How does Paul exonerate the law of Moses and show that the commandments are holy, just, and good?

- What difference does it make in my life that I have been brought from the old age of Adam to the new age of Christ?

Prayer

Lord Jesus, whose saving death and resurrection has brought me into a new spousal love with you, make me more aware of the power of sin and its luring enticements. Help me to live in the new life of the Spirit, bearing abundant fruit.

Wretched man that I am! Who will rescue me from this body of death? Thanks be to God through Jesus Christ our Lord! ROMANS 7:24–25

The Anguish of Sin's Enslavement

ROMANS 7:14–25 ¹⁴*For we know that the law is spiritual; but I am of the flesh, sold into slavery under sin.* ¹⁵*I do not understand my own actions. For I do not do what I want, but I do the very thing I hate.* ¹⁶*Now if I do what I do not want, I agree that the law is good.* ¹⁷*But in fact it is no longer I that do it, but sin that dwells within me.* ¹⁸*For I know that nothing good dwells within me, that is, in my flesh. I can will what is right, but I cannot do it.* ¹⁹*For I do not do the good I want, but the evil I do not want is what I do.* ²⁰*Now if I do what I do not want, it is no longer I that do it, but sin that dwells within me.*

²¹*So I find it to be a law that when I want to do what is good, evil lies close at hand.* ²²*For I delight in the law of God in my inmost self,* ²³*but I see in my members another law at war with the law of my mind, making me captive to the law of sin that dwells in my members.* ²⁴*Wretched man that I am! Who will rescue me from this body of death?* ²⁵*Thanks be to God through Jesus Christ our Lord!*

So then, with my mind I am a slave to the law of God, but with my flesh I am a slave to the law of sin.

Paul continues speaking in the first-person "I," but his language becomes increasingly personal, as he laments his own condition in solidarity with all of humanity. While continuing to uphold the law of Moses as holy, just, and good, he adds here that "the law is spiritual," suggesting that the law is given by inspiration and reflects God's will (verse 14). But he confesses that he himself is carnal, "of the flesh, sold into slavery under sin." Speaking about the human condition, Paul shows that the law informs us of our commitments before God, but it does not give us the ability to fulfill them. As good as the law is, it encounters people when they are already indwelt by sin and cannot free them from its slavery. Our sinful state only reveals the depth of our interior division, between willing and doing, between the mind and the flesh.

Paul admits that he is a mystery to himself: "I do not understand my own actions. For I do not do what I want, but I do the very thing I hate" (verse 15). Paul finds himself in that bewildering state with one foot in God's kingdom and the other in the world. He knows that there is a discernible good that he ought to do and that he wants to do, but he finds himself frustratingly unable to do it. His discernment over what is right confirms the goodness of the law, while his inability to do it confirms the power of sin (verse 16).

The human problem is that sin has set up house and lives within us (verses 17, 20). We are not the master of our own lives. Of course, Paul does not say that people are evil and can do no good. All people are capable of some good, and many people do great good. But the good we do is always less than what we ought to do and what we want to do. All of the great social evils of Paul's day and our own—like oppression, poverty, war, and consumerism—are only the multiplication and institutionalizing of the sin that resides within each person. Lasting transformation of culture must come from changes within the hearts of each person.

Paul is clear that the Christian life is one of struggle between the law of God that we know in our mind and the power of sin dwelling within us. The greatest saints, even more than most, have felt this maddening tension within themselves. It is the agony and ecstasy of the Christian life. But Paul's final word is not his anguished lament: "Wretched man that I am!" (verse 24). It is his grateful praise: "Thanks be to God through Jesus Christ our Lord!" (verse 25). It is amazing grace that saves the wretch. When little can be expected from humanity, everything may be hoped for from God. Although we make progress in our lives, the struggle with sin does not fade away. But our risen Lord gives forgiving grace for the present and salvation for the world to come.

Reflection and Discussion

- In what ways do I experience Paul's anguish in my own life?

- How might Christian faith and baptism have helped Paul with his struggle between his own will and the power of sin?

- Why do the lives of the saints express the anguish of this struggle even more intensely than most?

  S. Mother Teresa

Prayer

Thanks be to God through Jesus Christ our Lord, for you have rescued me from desolation and despair, and you have offered me forgiveness and hope. Send your Spirit to dwell within my being so that I may know your will and do what is good.

If the Spirit of him who raised Jesus from the dead dwells in you, he who raised Christ from the dead will give life to your mortal bodies also through his Spirit that dwells in you.
ROMANS 8:11

Choosing Life in the Spirit

ROMANS 8:1–17 ¹*There is therefore now no condemnation for those who are in Christ Jesus. ²For the law of the Spirit of life in Christ Jesus has set you free from the law of sin and of death. ³For God has done what the law, weakened by the flesh, could not do: by sending his own Son in the likeness of sinful flesh, and to deal with sin, he condemned sin in the flesh, ⁴so that the just requirement of the law might be fulfilled in us, who walk not according to the flesh but according to the Spirit. ⁵For those who live according to the flesh set their minds on the things of the flesh, but those who live according to the Spirit set their minds on the things of the Spirit. ⁶To set the mind on the flesh is death, but to set the mind on the Spirit is life and peace. ⁷For this reason the mind that is set on the flesh is hostile to God; it does not submit to God's law—indeed it cannot, ⁸and those who are in the flesh cannot please God.*

⁹But you are not in the flesh; you are in the Spirit, since the Spirit of God dwells in you. Anyone who does not have the Spirit of Christ does not belong to him. ¹⁰But if Christ is in you, though the body is dead because of sin, the Spirit is life because of righteousness. ¹¹If the Spirit of him who raised Jesus from the dead dwells in you, he who raised Christ from the dead will give life to your mortal bodies also through his Spirit that dwells in you.

[12]So then, brothers and sisters, we are debtors, not to the flesh, to live according to the flesh—[13]for if you live according to the flesh, you will die; but if by the Spirit you put to death the deeds of the body, you will live. [14]For all who are led by the Spirit of God are children of God. [15]For you did not receive a spirit of slavery to fall back into fear, but you have received a spirit of adoption. When we cry, "Abba! Father!" [16]it is that very Spirit bearing witness with our spirit that we are children of God, [17]and if children, then heirs, heirs of God and joint heirs with Christ—if, in fact, we suffer with him so that we may also be glorified with him.

Paul invites his hearers to rejoice in the new era of freedom and possibility that God has created "for those who are in Christ Jesus" (verse 1). He has made an emphatic break, signaled by the words "therefore now," from his preceding train of thought. For the law, which had been exploited by sin and condemned God's people to death, has been overcome by "the law of the Spirit of life in Christ Jesus" (verse 2). This liberating triumph is the result of God sending his Son "in the likeness of sinful flesh" to condemn sin (verse 3). He has done what neither the law nor the human will could accomplish. His redemptive and liberating work is extended to believers through the work of the Spirit in the community of faith. In this way, what God intended in the law of Moses can be fulfilled in us as we live in God's Spirit (verse 4).

Of course, the effects of sin in the world and in our own lives have not been destroyed. For those "outside" of Christ, sin still certainly prevails, and for those "in" Christ, we continue to experience the influences of sin as we journey to full salvation. But for those who live in faith and are baptized into Christ, the grip of the old era has been radically broken and we no longer live under sin's authority. In Jesus, God intervened to break the bondage of sin and to take personal responsibility for humanity's salvation. Now, God's Spirit is working to make Christ's victory over sin effective and internal in the lives of those who join their lives to him through faith.

Paul contrasts two opposite ways of life: life in the flesh, a way that is closed and hostile to God; and life in the Spirit, a way that is open and responsive to God (verses 5–6). The mindset of a person living in the flesh is motivated by self-centered interests and is oriented toward "death." The mindset of one living in the Spirit is empowered by God's liberating grace and is oriented toward "life and peace." There is, then, a tension in Christian life, and choices have to be made continually. But it is a constructive tension leading to growth and fuller life.

The Christian life is not just an agreement with the teachings of Jesus or an external identification with his cause; rather, it is an internal makeover in which the individual personally participates in divine life. It means allowing "the Spirit of him who raised Jesus from the dead" to live within us (verse 11). This vivifying energy of the Holy Spirit works within us not only in the present to reorient our lives, but continuously into the future, and ultimately will even transform our bodies, making them like the body of the risen Christ. The life we now share in the Spirit, though still influenced by sin and death, is the life that we will have in full at the final resurrection.

Paul contrasts the alienation and slavery caused by sin with the family created by the Spirit of God (verse 14). Sin abducts into fearful slavery; God adopts children into his own family (verse 15). As trusting and confident children, we able to call upon God as "Abba! Father!" With his Spirit within us, we share in all the privileges of Christ, becoming joint heirs of all the glory the Father has given the Son (verse 17).

Reflection and Discussion

- How do I tell whether I am living "in the flesh" or "in the Spirit"? What are the indicators of each in my own life?

- If Christ has condemned sin and freed me from its tyranny, why do I still experience the influence of sin?

- Since the Spirit works in the hearts of those who are committed to Christ in faith, how would I describe this internal work to another?

- What are some of the privileges and responsibilities of being children in the family of God?

Prayer

Spirit of God who raised Jesus from the dead, dwell in me and free me from the tyranny of sin. Make me a child of God, confident to call out "Abba!" and to know that God has given me an eternal inheritance.

If God is for us, who is against us? He who did not withhold his own Son, but gave him up for all of us, will he not with him also give us everything else? ROMANS 8:31–32

Confidence in the Victory of God's Love

ROMANS 8:18–39 ¹⁸*I consider that the sufferings of this present time are not worth comparing with the glory about to be revealed to us. ¹⁹For the creation waits with eager longing for the revealing of the children of God; ²⁰for the creation was subjected to futility, not of its own will but by the will of the one who subjected it, in hope ²¹that the creation itself will be set free from its bondage to decay and will obtain the freedom of the glory of the children of God. ²²We know that the whole creation has been groaning in labor pains until now; ²³and not only the creation, but we ourselves, who have the first fruits of the Spirit, groan inwardly while we wait for adoption, the redemption of our bodies. ²⁴For in hope we were saved. Now hope that is seen is not hope. For who hopes for what is seen? ²⁵But if we hope for what we do not see, we wait for it with patience.*

²⁶Likewise the Spirit helps us in our weakness; for we do not know how to pray as we ought, but that very Spirit intercedes with sighs too deep for words. ²⁷And God, who searches the heart, knows what is the mind of the Spirit, because the Spirit intercedes for the saints according to the will of God.

²⁸We know that all things work together for good for those who love God, who are called according to his purpose. ²⁹For those whom he foreknew he also predestined to be conformed to the image of his Son, in order that he might be the firstborn within a large family. ³⁰And those whom he predestined he also called;

and those whom he called he also justified; and those whom he justified he also glorified.

³¹*What then are we to say about these things? If God is for us, who is against us?* ³²*He who did not withhold his own Son, but gave him up for all of us, will he not with him also give us everything else?* ³³*Who will bring any charge against God's elect? It is God who justifies.* ³⁴*Who is to condemn? It is Christ Jesus, who died, yes, who was raised, who is at the right hand of God, who indeed intercedes for us.* ³⁵*Who will separate us from the love of Christ? Will hardship, or distress, or persecution, or famine, or nakedness, or peril, or sword?* ³⁶*As it is written,*

> *"For your sake we are being killed all day long;*
> *we are accounted as sheep to be slaughtered."*

³⁷*No, in all these things we are more than conquerors through him who loved us.* ³⁸*For I am convinced that neither death, nor life, nor angels, nor rulers, nor things present, nor things to come, nor powers,* ³⁹*nor height, nor depth, nor anything else in all creation, will be able to separate us from the love of God in Christ Jesus our Lord.*

Paul wants to share with us his understanding of God's saving plan for all of creation. We participate now in both the suffering and the glory of Christ, because we have been incorporated into him through the Holy Spirit. Yet, our sufferings now, though painfully real, are dwarfed by "the glory about to be revealed to us" (verse 18). In fact, all of creation longs with us for that glorious goal. Although the material world is now subject to corruption and decay, God has implanted within it the seed of hope, giving creation a natural urge and yearning for future glory (verses 19–21). Paul describes this longing of creation as "groaning in labor pains" (verse 22), waiting for the time of deliverance, like a mother in the pangs of birth yearning for the delivery of her child.

We too inwardly groan and wait, filled with patience and confident hope that God will bring what he has promised (verses 23–25). While we have received the grace of adoption into God's family at baptism, we await the full effect of that adoption with the bodily resurrection. Likewise, we have the "first fruits of the Spirit" now, confident that we will receive the full harvest of God's blessings to come. This divine Spirit adds his voice to the chorus of sighs and groans rising up to God as we struggle to pray (verses 26–27). God hears our feeble attempts at prayer because "the Spirit helps us in our weakness" and "intercedes for the saints," translating our moaning into filial petitions to the Father.

The final verses (verses 28–39) form a magnificent climax to the first half of Paul's letter as he celebrates the love of God, made visible in what Jesus Christ has done for humanity. We can have absolute confidence in our future because we know that it is in the hands of our all-powerful and all-loving God. Paul assures us that "all things work together for good" for those whose lives are enveloped in God's love (verse 28). God even uses our worst suffering for good purposes, for the sake of our salvation, the full realization of God's eternal plan for us. Our destiny is firmly set in God's purposes: to transform us into the glorified image of Christ and to bring us into the family of God forever (verses 29–30). Absolutely nothing can disturb that unshakable hope. Throughout the remainder of this jubilant passage, Paul sings of the victory that God has gained for humanity over all the powers that could conceivably oppose that love.

"God is for us" (verse 31)—this is the essence of the gospel Paul proclaims. As with all great truths, its articulation is disarmingly simple. With elevated eloquence, Paul praises God for his absolute faithfulness verified for the world in the person of Jesus Christ, "who died,...who was raised, who is at the right hand of God, who indeed intercedes for us" (verse 34). As the one who died, Jesus redeemed humanity from sin and judgment; as the one who was raised, he assures us of victory over death and the gift of eternal life. As the one at the right hand of God, Jesus reigns as Lord in power and glory. As the one who intercedes for us, the enthroned Lord exercises his authority on our behalf. Jesus assures us that God is for us, not only in his sacrificial love on the cross but also now in his sustaining love as our glorious Lord.

The faithfulness of God's love is extolled through six rhetorical questions (verses 31–35). The questions answer themselves and praise God, who is always with us. With God on our side, the forces that are marshaled against us cannot prevail. Since God even gave up his Son for our sake, paying the highest possible price, we can certainly trust God to give us everything we could possibly need (verse 32). Because the only one of any significance who could bring a charge against us or condemn us is the one who has done everything for us, then truly we have nothing to fear (verses 33–34). Since God has proven his love for us absolutely, we need never worry about any opposition.

Not even the greatest dangers and most painful experiences that humans could undergo can separate us from God's love (verses 35–36). Since God has made us "more than conquerors" (verse 37), having conquered the greatest of all enemies through Christ, we can live with absolute confidence that God is for us. Not even the strongest forces of the universe—earthly or cosmic, natural or supernatural, present or future—can separate us from God's love (verses 38–39). Paul uses all the fiercest terms he can imagine to show how ineradicable is the divine love that he has come to know through Jesus Christ.

Reflection and Discussion

- What is the difference between Christian hope and wishful thinking? How do Paul's words deepen the virtue of hope within me?

- Which of the threats mentioned in verses 35 and 38 are most real to me? Why can they not separate me from God's love?

Prayer

Lord Jesus Christ, who reigns in glory over all the powers of the world, assure me that nothing can separate me from the love of God, the divine devotion that is trustworthy in the midst of trials and suffering.

They are Israelites, and to them belong the adoption, the glory, the covenants, the giving of the law, the worship, and the promises; to them belong the patriarchs, and from them, according to the flesh, comes the Messiah. ROMANS 9:4–5

God's Sovereign Choice of the Israelites

ROMANS 9:1–18 ¹*I am speaking the truth in Christ—I am not lying; my conscience confirms it by the Holy Spirit—²I have great sorrow and unceasing anguish in my heart. ³For I could wish that I myself were accursed and cut off from Christ for the sake of my own people, my kindred according to the flesh. ⁴They are Israelites, and to them belong the adoption, the glory, the covenants, the giving of the law, the worship, and the promises; ⁵to them belong the patriarchs, and from them, according to the flesh, comes the Messiah, who is over all, God blessed forever. Amen.*

⁶*It is not as though the word of God had failed. For not all Israelites truly belong to Israel, ⁷and not all of Abraham's children are his true descendants; but "It is through Isaac that descendants shall be named for you." ⁸This means that it is not the children of the flesh who are the children of God, but the children of the promise are counted as descendants. ⁹For this is what the promise said, "About this time I will return and Sarah shall have a son." ¹⁰Nor is that all; something similar happened to Rebecca when she had conceived children by one husband, our ancestor Isaac. ¹¹Even before they had been born or had done anything good or bad (so that God's purpose of election might continue, ¹²not by works but by his call) she was told, "The elder shall serve the younger." ¹³As it is written,*

> "I have loved Jacob,
>   but I have hated Esau."

¹⁴*What then are we to say? Is there injustice on God's part? By no means!* ¹⁵*For he says to Moses,*

> "I will have mercy on whom I have mercy,
>   and I will have compassion on whom I have compassion."

¹⁶*So it depends not on human will or exertion, but on God who shows mercy.* ¹⁷*For the scripture says to Pharaoh, "I have raised you up for the very purpose of showing my power in you, so that my name may be proclaimed in all the earth."* ¹⁸*So then he has mercy on whomever he chooses, and he hardens the heart of whomever he chooses.*

In the first half of his letter (Rom 1—8), Paul has presented an inclusive account of the good news of Jesus Christ, demonstrating the faithfulness of God in offering salvation to both Jews and Gentiles on equal terms. He has first shown how all people—Jews and Gentiles alike—are alienated from God because of sin, and then how all people are bound together even more powerfully through the solidarity of grace, given in Jesus Christ to all who are joined to him in faith. The climactic conclusion of Paul's arguments so far, however, are overshadowed by a disturbing reality: the vast majority of the Jewish people have failed to respond in faith to the salvation offered through Jesus Christ. Thus, the gospel that Paul has presented so inclusively with respect to the Gentiles now seems to exclude the very people to whom God's promises were originally entrusted. Since the credibility of Paul's argument throughout his letter depends on the resolution of this dilemma, Paul devotes the next section of his letter (Rom 9—11) to explaining the relationship of Israel to the gospel, demonstrating how God is also acting inclusively with respect to the Jews.

Paul begins by expressing his anguished lament over the failure of his own people to receive Christ (verses 1–2). So inseparable is Paul from his own kindred that he states that, were it possible for him in any sense to do so, he would be willing to forfeit his own hope of salvation if it would gain theirs (verse 3). Yet, in the midst of his grief, he applauds eight unique blessings entrusted by God to Israel that mark them out as the people chosen for God's special purposes (verses 4–5). Although God has arrayed his own people with such magnificent gifts, Israel seems to have rejected its crown—the Messiah.

Paul then explains how the divided response of Israel to the Messiah continues a consistent pattern in salvation history. Although God has called and formed Israel into his own people through his word, Paul shows that "it is not as though the word of God had failed" (verse 6). Rather, Scripture demonstrates that the bearers and beneficiaries of God's promises have always been a chosen portion of the Israelites. Beginning with Abraham, God made limiting choices among his offspring. Although Abraham had many children, including Ishmael and six sons with Keturah after the death of Sarah (Gen 16:15; 25:1–2), his true descendants are named only through Isaac (verse 7). Likewise, within the next patriarchal generation, God shows his choice between Rebecca's twin sons, Esau and Jacob (verse 10). God reversed the natural order by announcing, "The elder shall serve the younger" (verse 12). God's election of Jacob was made before their birth, that is, before the children could do anything to earn or deserve God's choice. Through these examples from the patriarchs, Paul shows that "call" and "promise" determine the pattern of divine action, rather than ethnic belonging. God is free to pursue his own creative purposes independently of any contribution from the human side.

Lest the objection be raised that such divine choices constitute "injustice on God's part" (verse 14), Paul continues his explanation with illustrations from the book of Exodus, the first concerning Moses and the second concerning Pharaoh. Following Israel's rebellion against God at Mount Sinai, God affirms his character to Moses as one who shows mercy on those he wishes (verse 15; Exod 33:19). God is free to forgive as he wishes, even to show mercy to those who are undeserving of it. The second example demonstrates that God lifted up Pharaoh as his instrument in order to display his divine power and make known God's name throughout the earth (verse 17). God chose even Israel's arrogant oppressor to play a pivotal role in salvation's unfolding.

With all of these illustrations from Scripture, Paul begins to show how the present failure of God's people to recognize the Messiah could be part of God's inscrutable purposes. Israel's hardened heart might contain the seeds of God's saving design, the proclamation of God's name throughout all the earth.

Reflection and Discussion

- Why does Paul express such anguish over Israel's failure to receive the Messiah?

- What seems to be the main point in Paul's examples taken from the books of Genesis and Exodus?

- What are the implications of the biblical evidence that God often chooses the smaller, the weaker, and the younger over the bigger, the stronger, and the older?

  David.   - Goliath

Prayer

God of mercy and compassion, precious in your eyes are the despised and forgotten in the world. When I mistrust your justice and fail to understand your motivation, help me to realize that your will is always to bring people to salvation and the fullness of life.

Gentiles, who did not strive for righteousness,
have attained it, that is, righteousness through faith; but Israel,
who did strive for the righteousness that is based on the law,
did not succeed in fulfilling that law. ROMANS 9:30–31

The Divine Potter
and the Clay

ROMANS 9:19—10:4 ¹⁹*You will say to me then, "Why then does he still find fault? For who can resist his will?" ²⁰But who indeed are you, a human being, to argue with God? Will what is molded say to the one who molds it, "Why have you made me like this?" ²¹Has the potter no right over the clay, to make out of the same lump one object for special use and another for ordinary use? ²²What if God, desiring to show his wrath and to make known his power, has endured with much patience the objects of wrath that are made for destruction; ²³and what if he has done so in order to make known the riches of his glory for the objects of mercy, which he has prepared beforehand for glory—²⁴including us whom he has called, not from the Jews only but also from the Gentiles? ²⁵As indeed he says in Hosea,*

"Those who were not my people I will call 'my people,'
and her who was not beloved I will call 'beloved.'"

²⁶*"And in the very place where it was said to them, 'You are not my people,'*
there they shall be called children of the living God."

²⁷*And Isaiah cries out concerning Israel, "Though the number of the children of Israel were like the sand of the sea, only a remnant of them will be saved; ²⁸for the Lord will execute his sentence on the earth quickly and decisively." ²⁹And as Isaiah predicted,*

"If the Lord of hosts had not left survivors to us,
    we would have fared like Sodom
    and been made like Gomorrah."
[30]What then are we to say? Gentiles, who did not strive for righteousness, have attained it, that is, righteousness through faith; [31]but Israel, who did strive for the righteousness that is based on the law, did not succeed in fulfilling that law. [32]Why not? Because they did not strive for it on the basis of faith, but as if it were based on works. They have stumbled over the stumbling stone, [33]as it is written,
    "See, I am laying in Zion a stone that will make people stumble,
        a rock that will make them fall,
        and whoever believes in him will not be put to shame."

10 [1]Brothers and sisters, my heart's desire and prayer to God for them is that they may be saved. [2]I can testify that they have a zeal for God, but it is not enlightened. [3]For, being ignorant of the righteousness that comes from God, and seeking to establish their own, they have not submitted to God's righteousness. [4]For Christ is the end of the law so that there may be righteousness for everyone who believes.

Continuing to respond to possible objections from his hearers, Paul continues to clarify God's purposes, from the call of Abraham to the establishment of the church. Asking, "Who indeed are you, a human being, to argue with God?" Paul reminds his readers that the limitedness of human understanding cannot fathom the divine purpose. He employs the biblical image of the potter, illustrating the potter's freedom to shape vessels for any use. Like the potter, God orders times, events, and people for purposes of his choosing, some for "special use" and others for "ordinary use" (verse 21). The human creature has no right to complain about being made for one use and not another.

Having referred to Genesis and Exodus, Paul now continues his exposition of Scripture to demonstrate that God's way of proceeding is free and undetermined by human response. He now moves to the prophets and the time of Israel's exile. During this period, God has been reshaping his people, just as the potter remolds the clay. Indeed, God "has endured with much patience" those who have refused his saving will and made themselves "objects of wrath" (verse 22). Although God's wrath could have led God to make known his power, he has given them time to repent in hopes of showing them his mercy. For, in the present time of fulfillment, God is manifesting his glory upon those who are joining their lives to Christ and making themselves "objects of mercy" (verse 23).

Paul calls on passages from the prophets to show that God's call to both Jews and Gentiles is exactly what God intended according to his ancient design (verse 24). Although Hosea originally directed his words to the errant Israelites, Paul applies them to the Gentiles. Those who were formerly not God's people are now beloved "children of the living God" (verses 25–26). Moreover, Paul quotes Isaiah to show that God saves only a portion of his people, a "remnant" (verse 27) from among the numbers of Israel. For Paul, the remnant are those Jews who, like himself, have responded positively to the gospel. He is indicating that God is accomplishing his purposes now through a diminished Israel. But even a remnant is a testimony to God's grace. Had God not had mercy on the remnant, Israel's fate would have been total destruction, like that of Sodom and Gomorrah (verse 29).

The remnant of Israel, according to Paul, accounts for the relatively small number of the Jewish people responding to the gospel. However, the present remnant is not the end of God's plan. Paul wants his hearers to understand why Israel's failure has occurred and to do so as preparation for incorporating that temporary failure within a wider vision of God's saving purposes. He shows that those "who did not strive for righteousness" (justification; a right relationship with God) have attained it, while those "who did strive for righteousness" have not (verses 30–31). By receiving "righteousness through faith," the Gentiles have accepted the gift of salvation offered through God's Messiah. But, because the Jews believe that salvation is pursued through obeying the law of Moses, they have not been able to repent and receive God's saving grace. Paul describes this failure of Israel as a stumbling over the "stumbling stone," an image from Isaiah that Paul uses to refer to the crucified Messiah (verse 32).

Lamenting their lack of faith and inability to commit to their Messiah, Paul expresses his burning desire and prayerful wish that his people may be saved (10:1). He concedes that the Jewish people have a genuine "zeal for God," a kind of single-mindedness and unswerving loyalty to the God of the covenant (10:2). But he claims that their zeal is not enlightened, that it masks the bitter truth that Israel is a sinful people standing in need of the redemption offered by the crucified Messiah. Religious zeal can easily disguise the need for God's mercy, inhibiting the creative operation of God's grace. The root of Israel's failure is their attempt to establish, through the law of Moses, their own righteousness, rather than submitting to God's righteousness (10:3). For the righteousness given by God is received as grace by all who respond in faith, committing themselves to Christ. This is because Christ is "the end of the law"—not the termination of the law, but the completion of the saving work God has been doing through Israel. The law still stands, but it cannot be properly understood apart from Christ. The law is not the Savior. The law can diagnose sin, but only Christ can cure it.

Reflection and Discussion

- How much do I desire unbelievers to come to faith? How can my heart be more like that of Paul (10:1)?

- In what way can religious zeal stand in the way of growing in faith?

Prayer

Lord God, you are the potter and I am the clay being molded in your hands. Help me not to stumble, but to continually respond to your grace so that you may form me into the vessel you desire me to be.

SUGGESTIONS FOR FACILITATORS, GROUP SESSION 4

1. Welcome group members and ask if anyone has any questions, announcements, or requests.

2. You may want to pray this prayer as a group:

   Just and faithful God, who looks with compassion on the despised and forgotten of the world, rescue us from desolation and despair, give us forgiveness and hope, and assure us that no trials or suffering can separate us from your love. As children in your family, give us confidence to call out to you as Abba and to know that you have given us an eternal inheritance. Send your Spirit to dwell within us, so that we may know your will and do what is good, bearing abundant fruit in the world.

3. Ask one or more of the following questions:
   * What is the most difficult part of this study for you?
   * What insights stand out to you from the lessons this week?

4. Discuss lessons 13 through 18. Choose one or more of the questions for reflection and discussion from each lesson to discuss as a group. You may want to ask group members which question was most challenging or helpful to them as you review each lesson.

5. Keep the discussion moving, but allow time for the questions that provoke the most discussion. Encourage the group members to use "I" language in their responses.

6. After talking over each lesson, instruct group members to complete lessons 19 through 24 on their own during the six days before the next group meeting. They should write out their own answers to the questions as preparation for next week's session.

7. Ask the group what encouragement they need for the coming week. Ask the members to pray for the needs of one another during the week.

8. Conclude by praying aloud together the prayer at the end of one of the lessons discussed. You may choose to conclude the prayer by asking members to pray aloud any requests they may have.

There is no distinction between Jew and Greek; the same Lord is Lord of all and is generous to all who call on him. ROMANS 10:12

Israel's Response to the Gospel

ROMANS 10:5–21 ⁵*Moses writes concerning the righteousness that comes from the law, that "the person who does these things will live by them." ⁶But the righteousness that comes from faith says, "Do not say in your heart, 'Who will ascend into heaven?'" (that is, to bring Christ down) ⁷or 'Who will descend into the abyss?'" (that is, to bring Christ up from the dead). ⁸But what does it say?*

> *"The word is near you,*
> *on your lips and in your heart"*

(that is, the word of faith that we proclaim); ⁹because if you confess with your lips that Jesus is Lord and believe in your heart that God raised him from the dead, you will be saved. ¹⁰For one believes with the heart and so is justified, and one confesses with the mouth and so is saved. ¹¹The scripture says, "No one who believes in him will be put to shame." ¹²For there is no distinction between Jew and Greek; the same Lord is Lord of all and is generous to all who call on him. ¹³For, "Everyone who calls on the name of the Lord shall be saved."

¹⁴But how are they to call on one in whom they have not believed? And how are they to believe in one of whom they have never heard? And how are they to hear without someone to proclaim him? ¹⁵And how are they to proclaim him unless they are sent? As it is written, "How beautiful are the feet of those who bring good news!" ¹⁶But not all have obeyed the good news; for Isaiah says, "Lord, who has believed our message?" ¹⁷So faith comes from what is heard, and what is heard comes through the word of Christ.

[18]*But I ask, have they not heard? Indeed they have; for*
"Their voice has gone out to all the earth,
    and their words to the ends of the world."
[19]*Again I ask, did Israel not understand? First Moses says,*
  "I will make you jealous of those who are not a nation;
    with a foolish nation I will make you angry."
[20]*Then Isaiah is so bold as to say,*
  "I have been found by those who did not seek me;
    I have shown myself to those who did not ask for me."
[21]*But of Israel he says, "All day long I have held out my hands to a disobedient and*
contrary people."

Paul continues to contrast two kinds of righteousness: that which "comes from the law" and that which "comes from faith," asserting the efficacy of the latter in accordance with God's designs to make salvation universally obtainable in Christ (verses 5–6). He first cites the law of Moses to exemplify the old covenant: the one who keeps God's statutes and ordinances will live (Lev 18:5). But, as Paul has already demonstrated, it is not possible to attain righteousness by this means. In contrast, Paul finds in the same Torah the declaration of an alternative way of righteousness, based upon faith. In this passage, Moses speaks about the ease of responding to God's word (Deut 30:11–13). The word is not too difficult or too far away. We don't need to "ascend into heaven" because God has already sent his Son to us. We don't need to "descend into the abyss" because Christ has already died and risen for us. Indeed, "the word is near you, on your lips and in your heart" (verse 8; Deut 30:14). This "word of faith," as Paul interprets it in light of the new covenant, is the gospel of Jesus Christ. In contrast to righteousness that comes from the law, an effort doomed to frustration, this righteousness that comes from faith requires simply an acknowledgment of and submission to what God has already done.

Paul's summary of the way of justification by faith could be taken from an ancient confession used at baptism (verses 9–10). The proclamation that "Jesus is Lord," the earliest Christian creed, applies the personal name for God in the Torah to Jesus, acknowledging that he shares the dominion of Israel's God. So, to speak of Jesus is to speak of God. Since the lordship and resurrection of Jesus is the essence of the gospel, we receive the grace of salvation when we "confess" with our "lips" and "believe" in our "heart." The word of the gospel, "on your lips and in your heart," expresses the public witness and personal submission that genuine faith requires.

After instructing readers in the way of faith, Paul offers the words of the prophets to witness that the way of faith makes salvation open to believers on a universal scale (verses 11–13). Interpreting the words of Isaiah and Joel in light of the new covenant, Paul demonstrates that everyone who believes in Jesus as Lord and calls on his name will be saved. He concludes that this understanding signifies the solidarity of all believers, Jews and Gentiles, on the path to salvation. Just as all people were impoverished by sin, having no claim on salvation whatsoever, all people can now turn to the same Lord, who is "generous to all who call on him."

So how does Paul explain the failure of Israel to believe and proclaim that Jesus is Lord, opening the way to salvation in Christ? Who bears responsibility for this breakdown—God, the preachers of the gospel, or Israel? Paul formulates the steps preliminary to and required for Israel to "call" on the name of the Lord: calling presupposes believing, believing presupposes hearing, hearing presupposes someone to proclaim Christ, and proclaiming him presupposes someone who is sent (verses 14–15). In describing this process, Paul lists all the possible reasons Israel could have failed and then dismisses them one by one. The acts of announcing the gospel—sending and proclaiming—are the obligation of God and his missionaries. The words of Isaiah, "How beautiful are the feet of those who bring good news!" (verse 15; Isa 52:7), are fulfilled by ministers of the Christian gospel. But the acts of human response—hearing, believing, and calling on the Lord's name—have not been met with success on all fronts. As Paul laments, "Not all have obeyed the good news" or believed its message (verse 16).

Between proclaiming and believing the gospel comes the essential requirement of hearing. Has Israel heard the gospel? Paul's immediate answer, "Indeed they have," is enforced with a verse from a Psalm: "Their voice has gone out to all the earth, and their words to the ends of the world" (verse 18; Ps 19:4). The gospel has already been preached widely, from Jerusalem in the midst of Israel and out to the nations. Israel, of all nations, can hardly claim not to have heard.

Israel's final excuse, then, is that they have not understood God's plan as it culminated in the gospel (verse 19). But Paul quotes from Moses and the prophets to show that Israel must have understood. From the Torah, which says that God intends to make Israel "jealous" of "those who are not a nation," Paul sees a reference to the Gentiles. Turning to Isaiah 65:1–2, Paul contrasts the state of affairs between God and the Gentiles, on the one hand (verse 20), and God and Israel, on the other (verse 21). The Gentiles, who did not seek God or ask for him, have found God, and he has shown himself to them. But Israel, described by the prophet as "a disobedient and contrary people," have resisted God's appeal. They cannot plead lack of understanding. Israel is without excuse. But Israel's failure, in the context of God's wider purpose, is the springboard from which Paul will continue to unfold his vision of Israel's future salvation.

Reflection and Discussion

- What do these words from Deuteronomy mean to me in the context of Paul's teachings: "The word is near you, on your lips and in your heart"?

- What is the purpose of Paul's series of questions in verses 14–15? How do they apply to the church's call to missionary discipleship today?

Prayer

Lord Jesus, you have sent your missionary disciples to announce your gospel to the ends of the earth. Lead me to hear your word, believe in you, and call upon your name.

Inasmuch then as I am an apostle to the Gentiles, I glorify my ministry in order to make my own people jealous, and thus save some of them. ROMANS 11:13–14

God Has Not Rejected Israel

ROMANS 11:1–24 ¹*I ask, then, has God rejected his people? By no means! I myself am an Israelite, a descendant of Abraham, a member of the tribe of Benjamin.* ²*God has not rejected his people whom he foreknew. Do you not know what the scripture says of Elijah, how he pleads with God against Israel?* ³*"Lord, they have killed your prophets, they have demolished your altars; I alone am left, and they are seeking my life."* ⁴*But what is the divine reply to him? "I have kept for myself seven thousand who have not bowed the knee to Baal."* ⁵*So too at the present time there is a remnant, chosen by grace.* ⁶*But if it is by grace, it is no longer on the basis of works, otherwise grace would no longer be grace.*

⁷*What then? Israel failed to obtain what it was seeking. The elect obtained it, but the rest were hardened,* ⁸*as it is written,*

"God gave them a sluggish spirit,
eyes that would not see
and ears that would not hear,
down to this very day."

⁹*And David says,*

"Let their table become a snare and a trap,
a stumbling block and a retribution for them;
¹⁰*let their eyes be darkened so that they cannot see,*
and keep their backs forever bent."

¹¹*So I ask, have they stumbled so as to fall? By no means! But through their*

stumbling salvation has come to the Gentiles, so as to make Israel jealous. [12]Now if their stumbling means riches for the world, and if their defeat means riches for Gentiles, how much more will their full inclusion mean!

[13]Now I am speaking to you Gentiles. Inasmuch then as I am an apostle to the Gentiles, I glorify my ministry [14]in order to make my own people jealous, and thus save some of them. [15]For if their rejection is the reconciliation of the world, what will their acceptance be but life from the dead! [16]If the part of the dough offered as first fruits is holy, then the whole batch is holy; and if the root is holy, then the branches also are holy.

[17]But if some of the branches were broken off, and you, a wild olive shoot, were grafted in their place to share the rich root of the olive tree, [18]do not boast over the branches. If you do boast, remember that it is not you that support the root, but the root that supports you. [19]You will say, "Branches were broken off so that I might be grafted in." [20]That is true. They were broken off because of their unbelief, but you stand only through faith. So do not become proud, but stand in awe. [21]For if God did not spare the natural branches, perhaps he will not spare you. [22]Note then the kindness and the severity of God: severity toward those who have fallen, but God's kindness toward you, provided you continue in his kindness; otherwise you also will be cut off. [23]And even those of Israel, if they do not persist in unbelief, will be grafted in, for God has the power to graft them in again. [24]For if you have been cut from what is by nature a wild olive tree and grafted, contrary to nature, into a cultivated olive tree, how much more will these natural branches be grafted back into their own olive tree.

Since Paul has just shown how the Israelites seem to have rejected God's invitation to life in the Messiah and quoted the Torah and prophets to describe Israel as jealous, angry, disobedient, and contrary (10:19–21), he raises the question of God's faithfulness and reliability. In an attempt to include the Gentiles, has God excluded the Jews, his own covenanted people? Paul immediately answers the question with his characteristic "By no means!" (verse 1). For Paul, who is proud to identify himself as "an Israelite, a descendant of Abraham, a member of the tribe of Benjamin," the suggestion that God has rejected Israel is unthinkable.

Turning to the biblical story of Elijah hiding on Mount Horeb, Paul describes how the prophet complained to God against Israel: "Lord, they have killed your prophets, they have demolished your altars; I alone am left, and they are seeking my life" (verse 3; 1 Kings 19:10). Elijah felt that he was the last person left in Israel faithful to the Lord. But God corrects his impulse and states, "I have kept for myself seven thousand who have not bowed the knee to Baal" (verse 4; 1 Kings 19:18). Even if Elijah should die, God is not about to end his relationship with Israel. Although Paul might be tempted to make Elijah's complaint his own, Paul knows that God, in his mercy, has chosen a "remnant" as a sign of his continuing fidelity (verse 5). This remnant, consisting of Paul and all Jews who have abandoned seeking salvation through the law and have turned to God's Messiah, stands as a pledge that God has not rejected his own.

Asking the question, "What then?" (verse 7), Paul moves to the next stage of his response to the question, "Has God rejected his people?" He describes how Israel is divided into two groups: the Jewish Christian remnant, who have accepted God's saving grace through faith, and "the rest" of Israel, who have become "hardened" to God's invitation. Paul then adapts verses from the Torah, prophets, and psalms to reinforce his description of the hardening and "stumbling" of Israel (verses 8–10). The "sluggish spirit," the "stumbling block," the darkened eyes, and the bent backs of God's people emphasize that Israel's hardened state is a kind of resistance that inhibits a heartfelt response to God's grace. It is both humanly deserved and divinely imposed, the result of human defiance and divine discipline.

Referring to the hardened part of Israel, Paul asks, "Have they stumbled so as to fall?" (verse 11). He distinguishes between a stumbling that leads to a permanent, unrecoverable fall and a stumbling from which one can recover. Paul vigorously affirms the latter type of stumbling for Israel. This section of the letter shows that the stumbling occurs within God's broad purpose, encompassing both the salvation of the Gentiles and renewed hope for Israel. In fact, as Paul suggests, when the hardened and stumbling Israelites become aware of what the Gentiles have attained, they will become jealous and change their hearts, reversing their initial rejection and following the way to salvation. Paul admits to the Gentiles that his own mission as "apostle to the Gentiles" includes making his own people jealous so that they come to faith and salvation (verses 13–14). If Israel's temporary rejection has provided the opportunity for the gospel to be proclaimed throughout the Gentile world, imagine the benefits that will come with Israel's acceptance of the gospel! (verse 15). Paul offers two metaphors, the first fruits of the harvest and the roots of the olive tree, to emphasize how the holy beginnings of God's people in Israel make the whole church a holy offering to God (verse 16).

Paul develops his metaphor of the olive tree into an extended allegory for the people of the new covenant. He invites his listeners to visualize a cultivated olive tree with some of its branches broken off. In their place, shoots from a wild olive shrub have been grafted to the mature trunk, now drawing their sustenance from the tree's rich root (verse 17). Gentile believers, who now find themselves part of the people of God, are warned not to boast over their inclusion at the expense of unbelieving Jews. For, like the wild shoots supported now by the root, they have been added through God's mercy and have come to share in the graces God entrusted to Israel (verse 18). The Gentiles, then, ought to stand in awe of God, who is both kind—as they have experienced in being grafted to the tree—and severe—as the unbelieving Jews have experienced in being broken off from the tree (verses 20–22). For if God has broken off branches that naturally belong to the tree, how much easier would it be to break off the wild and grafted branches. The Gentiles must maintain a sense of humility and gratitude for the grace they have received and for the tradition of Israel in which they now stand.

With this allegory of the olive tree, Paul offers not only a warning for Gentiles, but the hope of salvation for all Israel. What is to be the fate of unbelieving Israel, the severed branches lying on the ground beneath the tree? Paul insists that Israel's hardening is not irreversible. If they do not persist in their unbelief, God will graft them back into their own olive tree (verses 23–24). If the wild olive branches that do not belong to the tree by nature can be grafted into the trunk, then how much more readily can branches that belong by nature to the tree's original stock be grafted back. The blessings of the covenant naturally belong to Israel, and God is not finished with Israel in fulfilling his purposes. The Gentiles, given access to the rich sap that runs through Israel from root to branch, now participate in the privilege of being God's people.

Reflection and Discussion

- In what ways does Paul feel like Elijah? What can I do when I feel like Elijah?

- In what ways did God stir up jealousy in the people of Israel? What was God's intention in provoking jealousy?

- What warning might Paul be offering to me through the analogy of the olive tree?

Prayer

Messiah and Lord, in your mercy you have grafted me as a wild branch to the cultivated tree of your people. Help me to persist in faith and live in you so that I may draw on the nourishing sap of your Holy Spirit.

As regards election they are beloved, for the sake of their ancestors; for the gifts and the calling of God are irrevocable. ROMANS 11:28–29

The Mystery of Salvation Revealed

ROMANS 11:25–36 ²⁵*So that you may not claim to be wiser than you are, brothers and sisters, I want you to understand this mystery: a hardening has come upon part of Israel, until the full number of the Gentiles has come in.* ²⁶*And so all Israel will be saved; as it is written,*

"Out of Zion will come the Deliverer;
he will banish ungodliness from Jacob."
²⁷*"And this is my covenant with them,*
when I take away their sins."

²⁸*As regards the gospel they are enemies of God for your sake; but as regards election they are beloved, for the sake of their ancestors;* ²⁹*for the gifts and the calling of God are irrevocable.* ³⁰*Just as you were once disobedient to God but have now received mercy because of their disobedience,* ³¹*so they have now been disobedient in order that, by the mercy shown to you, they too may now receive mercy.* ³²*For God has imprisoned all in disobedience so that he may be merciful to all.*

³³*O the depth of the riches and wisdom and knowledge of God! How unsearchable are his judgments and how inscrutable his ways!*

³⁴*"For who has known the mind of the Lord?*
Or who has been his counselor?"
³⁵*"Or who has given a gift to him,*
to receive a gift in return?"

³⁶*For from him and through him and to him are all things. To him be the glory forever. Amen.*

Addressing his "brothers and sisters," the new family of God consisting of both Gentiles and Jews who have accepted God's saving grace, Paul presents his final summary of God's plan that he has been developing throughout the letter (verse 25). He calls this divine plan the "mystery," by which he means the hidden plan of God that has now been unveiled in Jesus the Messiah. Mere human thinking is totally inadequate to understand how God is working his saving will in the world and could lead to the mistaken conclusion that God has disregarded Israel.

Stating the content of this mystery, Paul says that a period of "hardening" has come upon a substantial part of Israel so that most Jews, except for the remnant, have resisted a faithful response to God's grace. This hardening remains in place in order to allow time for the non-Jewish nations to accept the grace of salvation. Then, when the "full number" of the Gentiles has joined God's family through faith, "all Israel will be saved" (verse 26). Whether Paul has a specific number of saved Gentiles in mind or whether he is referring to a specific period of time is doubtful. Rather, Paul is revealing what he has discovered through Scripture to be the process for God's saving plan. "All Israel" refers here, as it does throughout the prophets, to all twelve tribes that have been exiled and scattered among the nations. Paul, then, is echoing one of the greatest divine promises in Scripture, that God will restore all the tribes of Israel in the Messiah. Since the great majority of Israel is dispersed into the peoples of the world, then the nations must be delivered in order for the tribes of Israel to be redeemed. In this way, God will bring all Israel to salvation by means of the Gentiles coming to salvation.

In a few short sentences, Paul concludes his summary of the mystery of God's saving plan for the world. Unbelieving Israelites stand before God in a paradoxical relationship: with regard to the preaching of the gospel, they are "enemies" of God's plan, but with regard to their covenant election, they are "beloved" (verse 28). Their obstruction of the gospel is for the sake of the Gentiles, who are given time for receiving salvation, but they are forever loved by God on account of their ancestors in the covenant. Even though much of Israel has rejected God's grace for a time, God has not rejected Israel. All Israel will be saved because of God's fidelity to his original call, so that Paul can boldly assert that "the gifts and the calling of God are irrevocable" (verse 29).

In its essence, the story of the world's salvation is an account of human disobedience overcome by divine mercy. Paul expresses the mercy of God at work in the experiences of the Gentiles and the Jews in this one symmetrical sentence: Just as the Gentiles were "once disobedient to God" but have "now received mercy" because of the disobedience of the Jews, so the Jews have "now been disobedient" in the interest of mercy for the Gentiles so that the Jews may, in time, receive mercy (verses 30–31). This expression of Paul's inclusive vision of the gospel confirms his earlier assertion: "Where sin abounded, grace abounds even more" (5:20). In Romans 1—8, he underlines the inclusion of the Gentiles; in Romans 9—11, he focuses on the inclusion of Israel. The God who demonstrated inclusive mercy upon the disobedient Gentiles will also draw disobedient Israel into the embrace of his inclusive mercy, so that God's salvation will be offered to all who call upon the name of the Lord and believe in him.

A remarkable hymn forms the conclusion of Paul's entire presentation up to this point. It is a beautiful combination of motifs from the Scriptures and Jewish tradition. The hymn is formed with a pattern of triads within a triad. First, it is divided into three basic units: the opening exclamation (verse 33), the rhetorical questions from Scripture (verses 34–35), and the concluding doxology (verse 36). The first unit praises the "depth" of three divine attributes: "the riches and wisdom and knowledge of God!" Together they extol the nature of God, which is beyond the grasp of human understanding. The second unit asks three rhetorical questions which, in reverse order, address the three divine attributes. Since God's "knowledge" is so broad, no one can know "the mind of the Lord." Because of God's profound "wisdom," no one can serve as his "counselor." And to one so "rich," there is no question of giving a gift to him so as "to receive a gift in return." The third unit opens with three prepositional phrases: "For from him and through him and to him are all things." All of creation, then, is gathered for one supreme purpose—to give glory to God forever. God, through his Messiah Jesus, has overcome the darkness created by human sin and is drawing together a united people—Jews and Gentiles—to give God glory, the only thing that humans may appropriately give to God.

Reflection and Discussion

- Paul asserts that "the gifts and the calling of God are irrevocable" (verse 29). In what ways is this assuring for Jews? How does it give confidence to the church?

Forgiveness leads to HOPE.

- How can the people of Israel be both enemies of God and beloved of God at the same time (verse 28)?

- Why does Paul choose to laud these particular traits of God as he concludes his exposition of the gospel (verse 33)?

Prayer

God of all the earth, how unfathomable is your wisdom as you reveal the mystery of your saving plan for the world. Thank you for calling me to life and showering me with your generous mercy and abundant grace.

Do not be conformed to this world, but be transformed by the renewing of your minds, so that you may discern what is the will of God—what is good and acceptable and perfect. ROMANS 12:2

Living as an Offering of Praise to God

ROMANS 12:1–8 *¹I appeal to you therefore, brothers and sisters, by the mercies of God, to present your bodies as a living sacrifice, holy and acceptable to God, which is your spiritual worship. ²Do not be conformed to this world, but be transformed by the renewing of your minds, so that you may discern what is the will of God— what is good and acceptable and perfect.*

³For by the grace given to me I say to everyone among you not to think of yourself more highly than you ought to think, but to think with sober judgment, each according to the measure of faith that God has assigned. ⁴For as in one body we have many members, and not all the members have the same function, ⁵so we, who are many, are one body in Christ, and individually we are members one of another. ⁶We have gifts that differ according to the grace given to us: prophecy, in proportion to faith; ⁷ministry, in ministering; the teacher, in teaching; ⁸the exhorter, in exhortation; the giver, in generosity; the leader, in diligence; the compassionate, in cheerfulness.

The final section of Paul's letter (Rom 12—16) begins with the small word "therefore," providing the transition and the essential connection between Paul's doctrinal teachings thus far and the pastoral concerns that follow. Here he summons all his hearers in the Christian community to a pattern of living in response to the gospel they have received. The grace that believers have been given in Christ is not an abstraction but a gift that gives shape and direction to Christian living. Paul exhorts the community to present their bodies as "a living sacrifice, holy and acceptable to God" (verse 1). Like the temple sacrifices given to God in worship, Christians are urged to offer their whole lives as a holy offering in worship of God.

In order to live the Christian life as a sacrificial consecration to God, Paul insists that his readers not be "conformed" to the world with all its superficial and passing attractions but be "transformed" by the power of grace to live in a new way of life (verse 2). God's transforming grace renews our minds, giving us the power to discern what is necessary to live according to "the will of God" in the often difficult and confusing situations we face in the world. The obedience of life flowing from that discernment makes of our lives a continual and "living sacrifice" that is acceptable and pleasing to God.

Like many Jews of his time, Paul understood that the world's history is divided into the present age, characterized by rebellion against God, and the age to come, in which God will give new life to the world, bringing joy, peace, and justice. Through his encounter with the risen Lord, Paul began to understand that the age to come was breaking into the present world through the death and resurrection of Jesus. For this reason, he challenges his listeners to discern how to think, speak, and act in a way that is countercultural, a way that is appropriate not for the world, but for the new age of the Messiah that has already begun.

Paul then begins to offer more detailed guidance for relationships within the Christian community (verses 3–8). Considering that faith and the spiritual gifts are a result of God's grace, believers must judge themselves and their gifts humbly in relationship to the community. The metaphor of the body expresses the ideal of a diversity of gifts within a unity of faith. As "one body in Christ," the church is made up of many members who have no need to compete with one another but who freely complement one another for the sake of the whole. Each member is given "gifts that differ according to the grace given to us" (verse 6). Offering a representative sample of these gifts and their functions, Paul emphasizes that they are not the possessions of the members but are endowments to be used for ministry within the community.

Reflection and Discussion

- When I think about my life as a living sacrifice to God, what implications arise for my daily living?

- What aspects of the present age must Christians set aside in order to be countercultural for the sake of God's kingdom among us?

- Part of a Christian's responsibility is to discover one's unique gift and then use it for the glory of God within the church. Which of the gifts listed in verses 6–8 are most like my gift? How can I put this to greater use for the good of others?

Prayer

Lord Jesus Christ, as we live in the light of your resurrection, we discover gifts from your Holy Spirit that are the result of divine grace working within us. Show me the gifts that are emerging within me and help me to use them for your church.

**Live in harmony with one another; do not be haughty,
but associate with the lowly; do not claim to be wiser than you are.**
ROMANS 12:16

Love in Action within the Church and the World

ROMANS 12:9–21 *⁹Let love be genuine; hate what is evil, hold fast to what is good; ¹⁰love one another with mutual affection; outdo one another in showing honor. ¹¹Do not lag in zeal, be ardent in spirit, serve the Lord. ¹²Rejoice in hope, be patient in suffering, persevere in prayer. ¹³Contribute to the needs of the saints; extend hospitality to strangers.*

¹⁴Bless those who persecute you; bless and do not curse them. ¹⁵Rejoice with those who rejoice, weep with those who weep. ¹⁶Live in harmony with one another; do not be haughty, but associate with the lowly; do not claim to be wiser than you are. ¹⁷Do not repay anyone evil for evil, but take thought for what is noble in the sight of all. ¹⁸If it is possible, so far as it depends on you, live peaceably with all. ¹⁹Beloved, never avenge yourselves, but leave room for the wrath of God; for it is written, "Vengeance is mine, I will repay, says the Lord." ²⁰No, "if your enemies are hungry, feed them; if they are thirsty, give them something to drink; for by doing this you will heap burning coals on their heads." ²¹Do not be overcome by evil, but overcome evil with good.

Through this series of exhortations, Paul offers a description of the Christian life as a holy and living sacrifice to God. They offer a no-nonsense vision of Christian living that is practical and challenging. Love heads the list and penetrates the entire sequence. Paul first describes love within the Christian community (verses 9–13) and then love within the wider society (verses 14–21). This love (*agape* in Greek) is a sacrificial, other-centered love, forming the lifeblood of the Christian way of life. This love is not shaped by the natural inclination of our fallen nature nor by the standards of the world but by the power of God's Spirit transforming the minds and wills of believers according to the standards of the new age in Christ.

Paul's advice on the love of Christians within the church is modeled on the affectionate love within families—the generous love of spouses and the patient care of siblings for one another. He says that this love must be "genuine," not hypocritical, not just for outward show (verse 9). Paul's admonition to "hate what is evil, hold fast to what is good" is steeped in the teachings of the prophet Amos, who urged his own generation to "hate evil and love good" (Amos 5:15). He promotes a practical charity between fellow disciples, encouraging them toward mutual affection and even a healthy competition at showing honor to others (verse 10). Continuing with encouraging words, he warns believers not to grow slack in their zeal but to remain fervent as they serve the Lord in season and out (verse 11). They must find joy in the hope of their salvation, remain steadfast in their times of suffering, and remain constant in a life of prayer (verse 12). Generosity to those in need and hospitality to travelers and foreigners complete Paul's description of a Christian community united in genuine love (verse 13).

Paul's counsel for Christian love within the wider world offers practical applications of Jesus' command to love one's enemies (Matt 5:44) and his call for nonretaliation in the face of opposition and persecution (Luke 6:28). Paul urges Christians facing persecution, verbal or physical, not to react in kind, but to invoke God's blessings on the offender (verse 14). Performing an act of kindness in exchange for an insult or abuse is radically different from our instinctual responses. But through the Spirit, God is transforming believers to receive, understand, and obey these teachings for life in the world. To bless our persecutors and not avenge our wrongs require the selflessness that only the power of God's love can bestow.

Christians living in the world should be good neighbors, prepared to rejoice when someone has good news and to be there to support and weep alongside those who face tragedy (verse 15). Living in accord with others, making company with the lowly, residing peaceably with all—this is the kind of simple witness that disciples of Jesus can offer daily to the world (verses 16–18). Paul commands believers, "Never avenge yourselves" (verse 19). Revenge keeps evil in circulation. Rather, "leave room for the wrath of God." God has his own ways of letting people experience the results of their own wickedness. The time and circumstances are not up to us. In contrast, Paul repeats an ancient proverb: "If your enemies are hungry, give them bread to eat; if they are thirsty, give them water to drink; for you will heap coals of fire on their heads" (Prov 25:21–22)—an expression that means bringing them to a burning sense of shame that can lead to a change of heart. The converted believer is able to discern God's will in all sorts of practical situations, learning how to "overcome evil with good" (verse 21), through union with the resurrected Lord and the power of his Spirit within.

Reflection and Discussion

- What does Paul mean when he says, "Let love be genuine" (verse 9)? How can I tell when my love is "genuine" and when it is "conformed to this world" (verse 2)?

- In what sense are Paul's exhortations contrary to our automatic, instinctual responses? What is required for us to be able to follow his appeals?

- Of all these exhortations, which ones are being followed best by my Christian community?

- Which three of these exhortations should I seek to practice during the coming week?

Prayer

Risen Lord, you call me to live in you, a life radically different from the life of the world. Guide me to discern in every instant how you desire me to live as your disciple, a life in the world but not of the world.

The night is far gone, the day is near. Let us then lay aside the works of darkness and put on the armor of light. ROMANS 13:12

Love Is the Fulfilling
of the Law

ROMANS 13:1–14 ¹*Let every person be subject to the governing authorities; for there is no authority except from God, and those authorities that exist have been instituted by God. ²Therefore whoever resists authority resists what God has appointed, and those who resist will incur judgment. ³For rulers are not a terror to good conduct, but to bad. Do you wish to have no fear of the authority? Then do what is good, and you will receive its approval; ⁴for it is God's servant for your good. But if you do what is wrong, you should be afraid, for the authority does not bear the sword in vain! It is the servant of God to execute wrath on the wrong-doer. ⁵Therefore one must be subject, not only because of wrath but also because of conscience. ⁶For the same reason you also pay taxes, for the authorities are God's servants, busy with this very thing. ⁷Pay to all what is due them—taxes to whom taxes are due, revenue to whom revenue is due, respect to whom respect is due, honor to whom honor is due.*

⁸Owe no one anything, except to love one another; for the one who loves another has fulfilled the law. ⁹The commandments, "You shall not commit adultery; You shall not murder; You shall not steal; You shall not covet"; and any other commandment, are summed up in this word, "Love your neighbor as yourself." ¹⁰Love does no wrong to a neighbor; therefore, love is the fulfilling of the law.

¹¹Besides this, you know what time it is, how it is now the moment for you to wake from sleep. For salvation is nearer to us now than when we became believers;

¹²the night is far gone, the day is near. Let us then lay aside the works of darkness and put on the armor of light; ¹³let us live honorably as in the day, not in reveling and drunkenness, not in debauchery and licentiousness, not in quarreling and jealousy. ¹⁴Instead, put on the Lord Jesus Christ, and make no provision for the flesh, to gratify its desires.

P aul continues his pastoral teachings, offering a delicate balance between the realities of the present age, in which Christians now live, and the demands of the age to come, which is already breaking in and transforming lives. Continuing to advise Christians to "discern what is the will of God" in every circumstance (12:2) and to "live in harmony" (12:16), his counsel includes good citizenship and cooperation in maintaining good order in society. While believers know that Jesus is now Lord of all, he wants them to understand that God has entrusted "governing authorities" to rule in the world (verses 1–2). Because all legitimate authority comes from God, Paul urges believers to submit to their civil rulers and not resist their governance. For civil authority serves as "God's servant," offering approval for good behavior and punishment for wrongdoing (verses 3–4).

The fact that Paul does not here raise the question of resistance to evil rulers or unjust governments cannot be interpreted to mean that he foresaw no circumstances where resistance might be justified. But, in writing to inhabitants of the empire's capital, he wisely chose to discuss the subject from the ideal rather than from its possible exceptions. Many Jews of the time regarded submission to foreign powers as a violation of their status of God's people, a position that led to frequent rebellions against their Roman overlords. Since the emperor had recently expelled the Jews from Rome, Paul does not want the Christian community to incur the emperor's wrath or to receive a reputation as troublemakers inciting civil unrest.

Submission to legitimate authorities, Paul teaches, should be motivated not only by fear of punishment but also by "conscience" (verse 5). This submission is not blind obedience without regard to moral responsibility. The inner management of conscience should guide the discernment of Christians as they consider their own responsibilities regarding their behavior in society. So, as a general rule, Christians should "pay to all what is due to them," whether it be taxes, revenue, respect, or honor to the authorities who serve as "God's servants" (verses 6–7). In the present age, believers cannot withdraw from civil responsibility but are accountable to it. They are not called to subvert the present order but to sanctify it, promoting the betterment of society, bringing its laws and practices into alignment with the gospel.

Paul broadens his message to declare that there is one debt, beyond all the obligations of citizenship, which can never be paid in full. The inexhaustible love believers have received through Christ has created a "debt" of love owed to fellow human beings (verse 8). The commandments he cites are prohibitions, forbidding actions that would harm the neighbor (verse 9). Paul is suggesting that the commandments of the law restrain harmful action, whereas love penetrates to the intent of the law, fulfilling the law's requirements and going beyond them. For this reason, Paul declares, like Jesus, that they are all summed up in the command, "Love your neighbor as yourself" (verse 9; Lev 19:18). Both the law and the gospel direct God's people to the same goal. Those who truly love in this way fulfill all the commandments of the law. No domain of Christian life, including the sphere of civic duties, stands apart from this all-enfolding responsibility.

Paul concludes this section of his pastoral teachings by appealing to the urgency of the moment with the image of a person waking from sleep at the onset of dawn (verse 11). It is time to put off the slumber attached to the present age and to wake up to the new age that is dawning. Since Christian existence belongs to the day and not the night, it is time to change clothes, casting aside "the works of darkness" and putting on "the armor of light" (verse 12). This armor equips the believer for battle against the demonic forces ruling the present age, which will not give in without a struggle. The clothing image continues with the baptismal exhortation: "Put on the Lord Jesus Christ" (verse 14). Through faith and baptism, his character becomes our character, his way becomes our path forward, and his promises for the future become our certain hope.

Reflection and Discussion

- How does a Christian determine whether to submit to the decrees of a civil authority or to resist them?

- What are Christians to do when rulers trample on human rights or interfere with the practice of the faith? What times and places in history can serve as models for nonviolent resistance?

- What serves as my "armor of light"?

Prayer

Risen Lord, you lead us to the new day of salvation as we cast off deeds of darkness and put on the armor of light. Continue to guide me into the future, from the day I first believed to the fullness of salvation that you have promised me.

SUGGESTIONS FOR FACILITATORS, GROUP SESSION 5

1. Welcome group members and ask if anyone has any questions, announcements, or requests.

2. You may want to pray this prayer as a group:

   God of all the earth, how unfathomable is your wisdom as you reveal the mystery of your saving plan for the world. As you have grafted us as a wild branch to the cultivated tree of your people Israel, may we unite our lives with Jesus the Messiah and draw on the nourishing sap of the Holy Spirit. As we live in the light of the resurrection, give us the desire to live as disciples of Jesus, a life radically different from the life of the world. Lead us to discover the gifts of the Holy Spirit that are the result of your grace, and show us how to use them for your church.

3. Ask one or more of the following questions:
   - What most intrigued you from this week's study?
   - What makes you want to know and understand more of God's word?

4. Discuss lessons 19 through 24. Choose one or more of the questions for reflection and discussion from each lesson to talk over as a group.

5. Ask the group members to name one thing they have most appreciated about the way the group has worked during this Bible study. Ask group members to discuss any changes they might suggest in the way the group works in future studies.

6. Invite group members to complete lessons 25 through 30 on their own during the six days before the next meeting. They should write out their own answers to the questions as preparation for next week's session.

7. Ask group members how their study of Romans has helped them understand how the church is both worldwide and local as well as both unified and diverse. Discuss some of these insights.

8. Conclude by praying aloud together the prayer at the end of one of the lessons discussed. You may want to conclude the prayer by asking members to voice prayers of thanksgiving.

If we live, we live to the Lord, and if we die, we die to the Lord;
so then, whether we live or whether we die, we are the Lord's.

ROMANS 14:8

Fostering Unity without Imposing Uniformity

ROMANS 14:1–12 ¹*Welcome those who are weak in faith, but not for the purpose of quarreling over opinions. ²Some believe in eating anything, while the weak eat only vegetables. ³Those who eat must not despise those who abstain, and those who abstain must not pass judgment on those who eat; for God has welcomed them. ⁴Who are you to pass judgment on servants of another? It is before their own lord that they stand or fall. And they will be upheld, for the Lord is able to make them stand.*

⁵Some judge one day to be better than another, while others judge all days to be alike. Let all be fully convinced in their own minds. ⁶Those who observe the day, observe it in honor of the Lord. Also those who eat, eat in honor of the Lord, since they give thanks to God; while those who abstain, abstain in honor of the Lord and give thanks to God.

⁷We do not live to ourselves, and we do not die to ourselves. ⁸If we live, we live to the Lord, and if we die, we die to the Lord; so then, whether we live or whether we die, we are the Lord's. ⁹For to this end Christ died and lived again, so that he might be Lord of both the dead and the living.

¹⁰Why do you pass judgment on your brother or sister? Or you, why do you

despise your brother or sister? For we will all stand before the judgment seat of God. [11]*For it is written,*
> *"As I live, says the Lord, every knee shall bow to me,*
> *and every tongue shall give praise to God."*
[12]*So then, each of us will be accountable to God.*

In order to foster unity in the church, Paul urges Christians to be tolerant of the differing "opinions" among themselves and to welcome one another. He describes these differences of opinion as matters regarding Jewish dietary rules (verse 2) and observing feast days of the Jewish calendar (verse 5). The congregation seems to be split into two groups, whom Paul calls the "weak" and the "strong," with both sides holding firm convictions about their views. The weak, according to Paul, are those who have not allowed their faith in Christ to permeate all areas of life, so they insist on the kosher practices and other regulations of the Mosaic law. The strong are those who, like himself, have grown to understand that all foods are now clean and to fully accept their freedom in Christ. The weak continue to follow a traditional Jewish way of life, while the strong believe that Judaism's ritual observances are non-issues for Christians.

The tensions within the church of Rome were aggravated by the historical situation. The expulsion of all Jews and Jewish Christians from Rome in A.D. 49 left only Gentile Christians to develop their own understanding of the gospel. When Claudius died and Jewish Christians gradually returned to the city, they brought with them their more legalistic understanding of faith. Many among those weak in faith would insist, for example, on eating only vegetables, perhaps because it was difficult to obtain kosher meats in Rome. Paul is concerned with the pastoral fallout from these strained conditions and wants the factions to worship together. Addressing the "strong," Paul insists that "those who eat must not despise those who abstain," suggesting that the strong had adopted a condescending attitude toward the weak (verse 3). Then, addressing the "weak," he asserts that "those who abstain must not pass judgment on those who eat." They are free to maintain their dietary customs so deeply rooted in their Jewish tradition, but they must not be openly critical of the strong and judge their commitment to the Lord.

Just as a servant has no authority to pass judgment on a fellow servant, so also a Christian must not judge another Christian (verse 4). Only the master and Lord possesses this authority. With this analogy, Paul urges the believers in the church to look beyond their differences and maintain harmony within the community. He is confident that both the weak and the strong act with the same motive in mind: they seek to honor the Lord and give thanks to God (verse 6). Therefore, they must not try to impose uniformity in non-essential concerns but allow for diversity of opinion and practice on matters that are not at the core of their unity in Christ.

As Christians, we are not the masters of our own lives: "We do not live to ourselves, and we do not die to ourselves" (verse 7). At whatever stage of life's pilgrimage we are experiencing, whether we are living or dying, "we are the Lord's" (verse 8). Christ, who died and rose to life, is the Lord of both the dead and the living (verse 9). From the perspective of "the judgment seat of God," the importance of special diets and special days seems insignificant (verse 10). Far more important is the peril that faces Christians who pass judgment of their brother or sister or who despise one another.

Reflection and Discussion

- Be united in things essential for faith, tolerant in things not essential, and wise in knowing the difference between them. How could this instruction guide Christian communities today?

- Why does Paul urge the Christians of Rome not to judge one another?

- What is the difference between unity and uniformity? How can diversity of opinion and practice be beneficial for the church?

- Over what issues in our own day are we in danger of judging one another because of things Paul would declare to be indifferent?

Prayer

Lord our God, every knee shall bow to you and every tongue give you praise. Let the perspective of your rule and judgment teach me what is essential and what is trivial on my pilgrimage of life.

Do not let your good be spoken of as evil.
For the kingdom of God is not food and drink but righteousness
and peace and joy in the Holy Spirit. ROMANS 14:16–17

Freedom in Service of Love

ROMANS 14:13–23 ¹³*Let us therefore no longer pass judgment on one another, but resolve instead never to put a stumbling block or hindrance in the way of another. ¹⁴I know and am persuaded in the Lord Jesus that nothing is unclean in itself; but it is unclean for anyone who thinks it unclean. ¹⁵If your brother or sister is being injured by what you eat, you are no longer walking in love. Do not let what you eat cause the ruin of one for whom Christ died. ¹⁶So do not let your good be spoken of as evil. ¹⁷For the kingdom of God is not food and drink but righteousness and peace and joy in the Holy Spirit. ¹⁸The one who thus serves Christ is acceptable to God and has human approval. ¹⁹Let us then pursue what makes for peace and for mutual upbuilding. ²⁰Do not, for the sake of food, destroy the work of God. Everything is indeed clean, but it is wrong for you to make others fall by what you eat; ²¹it is good not to eat meat or drink wine or do anything that makes your brother or sister stumble. ²²The faith that you have, have as your own conviction before God. Blessed are those who have no reason to condemn themselves because of what they approve. ²³But those who have doubts are condemned if they eat, because they do not act from faith; for whatever does not proceed from faith is sin.*

Paul continues to address ways of promoting tolerance motivated by love for fellow Christians. Although Christians are free from the legal restraints of the law, they have a responsibility to use their freedom in a way that builds up rather than tears down the church's unity. Not only must they not judge one another, they must resolve "never to put a stumbling block or hindrance in the way of another" (verse 13). When believers act selfishly with regard to freedom, their actions may create a stumbling block in the path of another, causing the other to trip and fall in the way of faith. Likewise, believers can create a hindrance that entices others to act against their conscience. Such irresponsible choices can scandalize others, jeopardizing their developing faith and threatening their relationship with the community.

The example Paul uses is again the issue of Jewish dietary regulations. Although he has come to the personal conviction that "nothing is unclean in itself" and no food is forbidden from consumption, the weak in faith remain convinced that some foods are legally unclean and should not be eaten (verse 14). What determines the rightness or wrongness of a particular action is not just the objective order, but the understanding and disposition of the subject as well. For this reason, Paul urges the strong in faith to be tolerant of the weak by following Jewish dietary laws when dining in their company. He declares, "If your brother or sister is being injured by what you eat, you are no longer walking in love" (verse 15). A decision about what to eat should not be determined by what one is able to do in freedom but what one ought to do in love for the other. A believer can never look upon another Christian in any way other than as one whom Christ loved even unto death. This view of brothers and sisters in Christ confers on them a value that overwhelms any selfish consideration.

The promotion of tolerance and harmony within the community concerns not only relationships among believers but also witness to the unbelieving world. If disputes over food and drink lead to divisions among Christians, the gospel will be discredited among the population of Rome. The Christians in Rome must be witnesses of "the kingdom of God," the divine reign established in Jesus the Messiah, which is manifested through gifts of the Holy Spirit: "righteousness and peace and joy" (verse 17). Righteousness is the grace of justification given to the believer; peace is the reconciliation that reunites the believer in the family of God; and joy is the delight in God's goodness present in the believer's heart. These are the signs now present in the Christian community, foretastes of the full salvation that believers await. In comparison to these blessings, such matters as the freedom to eat and drink fade into insignificance. In no way do these issues belong to the essence of God's kingdom.

Paul thus urges the Christians in Rome to set priorities, to pursue what really matters, to build up the church, and to establish sacrificial love of neighbor as the overriding concern. The one who "serves Christ" in this way can expect a favorable verdict at the final judgment and serves as a witness of the gospel to unbelieving Rome (verse 18). Again, Paul asserts that a Christian must be willing to refrain from doing something that is permissible in faith because it is not responsible in love. Christians must hold fast to their convictions, not bending under the weight of social pressures, because acting against convictions is acting against conscience (verses 22–23). Christian freedom is genuine only when it flows from the sense that one is guarding against scandalizing another, giving poor witness to the world, or transgressing one's conscience.

Reflection and Discussion

- What can I do to "pursue what makes for peace and for mutual upbuilding" (verse 19) in my community?

- We must learn to bear with the weaknesses of others, just as Christ gave himself up for us in our weakness. How can I grow in sensitivity for the weaknesses of others?

love is willing the good of others

Prayer

Merciful God, send your Holy Spirit upon me with gifts of righteousness, peace, and joy. Guide me in my choices so that I use my freedom well, setting priorities rightly, serving as an example to others, and building up your church.

**May the God of steadfastness and encouragement grant you
to live in harmony with one another, in accordance with Christ Jesus,
so that together you may with one voice glorify the God and
Father of our Lord Jesus Christ.** ROMANS 15:5–6

Christ as Model of Tolerance and Unity

ROMANS 15:1–13 ¹*We who are strong ought to put up with the failings of the weak, and not to please ourselves.* ²*Each of us must please our neighbor for the good purpose of building up the neighbor.* ³*For Christ did not please himself; but, as it is written, "The insults of those who insult you have fallen on me."* ⁴*For whatever was written in former days was written for our instruction, so that by steadfastness and by the encouragement of the scriptures we might have hope.* ⁵*May the God of steadfastness and encouragement grant you to live in harmony with one another, in accordance with Christ Jesus,* ⁶*so that together you may with one voice glorify the God and Father of our Lord Jesus Christ.*

⁷*Welcome one another, therefore, just as Christ has welcomed you, for the glory of God.* ⁸*For I tell you that Christ has become a servant of the circumcised on behalf of the truth of God in order that he might confirm the promises given to the patriarchs,* ⁹*and in order that the Gentiles might glorify God for his mercy. As it is written,*

"Therefore I will confess you among the Gentiles,
   and sing praises to your name";
¹⁰*and again he says,*
   "Rejoice, O Gentiles, with his people";

¹¹*and again,*
> *"Praise the Lord, all you Gentiles,*
> > *and let all the peoples praise him";*

¹²*and again Isaiah says,*
> *"The root of Jesse shall come,*
> > *the one who rises to rule the Gentiles;*
> *in him the Gentiles shall hope."*

¹³*May the God of hope fill you with all joy and peace in believing, so that you may abound in hope by the power of the Holy Spirit.*

Continuing his discussion of the strong and weak in faith, Paul again emphasizes that strength is a privilege that carries a responsibility. The strong ought to tolerate the failings of the weak, turning away from their own legitimate freedoms and selfish interests in order to care for their neighbors and build them up in their commitment to the gospel (verses 1–2). In this way, Christians follow the sacrificial pattern set by Christ, who gave up any claim of privilege and exposed himself to derision culminating at the cross (verse 3).

Paul's quotation from the psalms of Israel reinforces his counsel for Christians to take on the self-emptying of Christ: "The insults of those who insult you have fallen on me" (Ps 69:9). Like other New Testament writers, Paul reads the psalms through the lens of Christian faith and regards Jesus as the subject. Here he envisions Jesus as the speaker of these words, reminding the strong of the afflictions endured by the Messiah for his devotion to God's mission. Paul is suggesting that the strong, if they adapt their ways to the needs of the weak and care for them, risk exposing themselves to the ridicule of the world. This understanding of Scripture—that the ancient texts are to be read in the light of Christ and "whatever was written in former days was written for our instruction"—means that Christians can look confidently to any passage to provide them with encouragement and hope (verse 4). This passage from Psalm 69, then, offers Christians reassurance through the sacrifices they endure for the sake of the weak because they are bearing them in union with Christ.

Although Paul teaches that diversity is expected within the church— between the weak and the strong, between Jews and Gentiles—he implores the community to "live in harmony" so that they may glorify God "with one voice" (verses 5–6). This unity of witness and worship demonstrates, both to the watching world and to Christians themselves, that they are not revering one of the many ethnic gods of the culture but the one God of all the world, now proclaimed as "the God and Father of our Lord Jesus Christ."

As Paul concludes the teaching part of his letter, he summarizes what he has been illuminating throughout the letter and what the whole Old Testament was moving toward. God has brought the nations of the world into unity with his chosen people, Israel (verse 8). Gentiles must understand that their salvation comes through the patriarchs of Israel, and Jews must understand that God's promise to Israel from the beginning included the Gentiles. The assorted quotations from the Torah, prophets, and psalms (verses 9–12) show that God always intended to bring all people—Jews and Gentiles— together in unity. These Scriptures, along with all the ancient texts, can now be read not as a puzzling story in search of an ending but as the foundation of God's great achievement in Jesus Christ. This string of triumphant passages draws Paul's teaching to a close by summarizing God's purposes in bringing Jews and Gentiles into a single family. What God has already accomplished in Jesus on the cross, God will bring to completion throughout the world through the worship and witness of the church.

Reflection and Discussion

- How does Paul's use of the Old Testament help me understand its fuller purpose in the light of Christ?

- Why does Paul encourage a lifestyle of putting others first? How has my sensitivity to the consciences of others developed with my growth in faith?

- Why is it so critically important that Christians work together toward unity in Christ?

- In what ways do verses 7–13 provide a summary and conclusion of all that Paul has taught in his Letter to the Romans?

Prayer

God of steadfastness and encouragement, grant me to live in harmony with others in Christ, so that we may glorify you with one voice. Fill me with joy and peace in believing, so that I may abound in hope by the power of the Holy Spirit.

I have written to you rather boldly by way of reminder,
because of the grace given me by God to be a minister of Christ Jesus
to the Gentiles in the priestly service of the gospel of God.
ROMANS 15:15–16

Paul's Evangelizing Mission

ROMANS 15:14–33 ¹⁴*I myself feel confident about you, my brothers and sisters, that you yourselves are full of goodness, filled with all knowledge, and able to instruct one another. ¹⁵Nevertheless on some points I have written to you rather boldly by way of reminder, because of the grace given me by God ¹⁶to be a minister of Christ Jesus to the Gentiles in the priestly service of the gospel of God, so that the offering of the Gentiles may be acceptable, sanctified by the Holy Spirit.*

¹⁷In Christ Jesus, then, I have reason to boast of my work for God. ¹⁸For I will not venture to speak of anything except what Christ has accomplished through me to win obedience from the Gentiles, by word and deed, ¹⁹by the power of signs and wonders, by the power of the Spirit of God, so that from Jerusalem and as far around as Illyricum I have fully proclaimed the good news of Christ. ²⁰Thus I make it my ambition to proclaim the good news, not where Christ has already been named, so that I do not build on someone else's foundation, ²¹but as it is written,

"Those who have never been told of him shall see,

and those who have never heard of him shall understand."

²²This is the reason that I have so often been hindered from coming to you. ²³But now, with no further place for me in these regions, I desire, as I have for many years, to come to you ²⁴when I go to Spain. For I do hope to see you on my journey and to be sent on by you, once I have enjoyed your company for a little while. ²⁵At present, however, I am going to Jerusalem in a ministry to the saints; ²⁶for Macedonia and

Achaia have been pleased to share their resources with the poor among the saints at Jerusalem. [27]*They were pleased to do this, and indeed they owe it to them; for if the Gentiles have come to share in their spiritual blessings, they ought also to be of service to them in material things.* [28]*So, when I have completed this, and have delivered to them what has been collected, I will set out by way of you to Spain;* [29]*and I know that when I come to you, I will come in the fullness of the blessing of Christ.*

[30]*I appeal to you, brothers and sisters, by our Lord Jesus Christ and by the love of the Spirit, to join me in earnest prayer to God on my behalf,* [31]*that I may be rescued from the unbelievers in Judea, and that my ministry to Jerusalem may be acceptable to the saints,* [32]*so that by God's will I may come to you with joy and be refreshed in your company.* [33]*The God of peace be with all of you. Amen.*

Paul demonstrates here both his missionary passion and pastoral devotion. Diplomatically he expresses his confidence in the Roman community of believers for possessing the goodness and knowledge required to instruct one another as they develop as the church (verse 14). However, because of his responsibilities before God, he has written to them "rather boldly" as a reminder of the gospel they already know (verse 15). Paul then beautifully expresses his understanding of his apostolic calling in the language of liturgical worship. He realizes that he is fulfilling God's commission to Israel as a "minister of Christ Jesus to the Gentiles" (verse 16). He saw himself as a priest through whom "the offering of the Gentiles" was being brought before God. Previously considered ritually unclean and denied access to God's presence in the temple, the Gentiles are now brought by Paul as a truly acceptable offering, "sanctified by the Holy Spirit."

In reviewing the achievements of his life's work for God, Paul states that he has reason to "boast," but only in "what Christ has accomplished" through him (verses 17–18). He himself is not the source of salvation for the Gentiles; he is only the vessel of the signs and wonders accomplished "by the power of the Spirit of God" (verse 19). His missionary proclamation of the gospel has brought him along the whole eastern seaboard of the Mediterranean, from Jerusalem to Illyricum, an area comprised of today's Balkan Peninsula on the east coast of the Adriatic Sea.

Paul's missionary strategy along this vast arc of evangelization has been the maximum spread of the gospel in the minimum amount of time. He has focused on proclaiming the good news to Gentile nations previously untouched by Christian preaching or knowledge of the Jewish Messiah. He sees his own career reflected in a prophecy from Isaiah, bringing the good news of Christ "to those who have never been told of him" (verse 21; Isa 52:15). Paul has certainly not preached everywhere and to everyone in these regions. His strategy, rather, has been to establish Christianity in the urban centers and then to allow his converts to evangelize outlying areas. He lays the foundation for the church; then others build on the foundation as the church in each area grows and matures.

Paul now stands on the threshold of a new stage in his missionary career. Having evangelized the eastern parts of the Roman Empire, he sets his sights on its westernmost limit—Spain (verses 23–24). On his journey westward, Paul hopes to stay "for a little while" in Rome, a city with a Christian community he has desired to visit for many years. But before he travels westward, he must first go eastward again to Jerusalem. There Paul intends to deliver a financial contribution he has collected on his journeys for the needs of the poor in Jerusalem (verses 25–26). He describes this collection as a kind of debt that Gentiles owe to Jews. As Paul explains it, the Gentiles have come to share in the "spiritual blessings" of Israel, represented by the Jewish Christians in Jerusalem. This privilege of having shared the blessings of Israel creates a responsibility to share with the Jews in Jerusalem in their material needs (verse 27). So, the collection is a tangible expression of solidarity among Gentiles and Jews in the growing worldwide church. It demonstrates to Gentile Christians that their roots are in Israel; it demonstrates to Jewish Christians that their Messiah is the one Lord of Gentiles as well.

Paul anticipates his journey to Jerusalem with much apprehension. He knows that there are some among the unbelieving Jews who are seeking his life, seeing him as a traitor who has led Israel astray. He is also anxious about how his collection will be received by the Jewish Christians, for their acceptance will express their recognition of Gentile Christians as sharers in the family of God. Paul is literally risking his life for the unity of the church. So he requests prayers of the Christians in Rome for his journey. Then, if all goes well, he will come to visit Rome "with joy" after his ministry in Jerusalem and before his missionary journey to Spain. Paul says nothing more about his plans, but clearly, they reflect the twin concerns of his life: his fidelity to the Jewish origins of the church in Jerusalem and his missionary calling to the ends of the earth.

Reflection and Discussion

- How does Paul understand his ministry to the Gentiles as "priestly service"?

- Besides relieving the poor in their needs, why is the collection for Jerusalem so important to Paul?

- What characteristics of Paul's plans and ambitions would I like to incorporate into my own life?

Prayer

God of peace, who has reconciled Jews and Gentiles and joined them together as your people, teach me to build bridges to people different from myself, and so do my part to create solidarity and unity among the peoples of your church.

Greet one another with a holy kiss.
All the churches of Christ greet you. ROMANS 16:16

Paul's Greetings to the Saints in Rome

ROMANS 16:1–16 ¹*I commend to you our sister Phoebe, a deacon of the church at Cenchreae, ²so that you may welcome her in the Lord as is fitting for the saints, and help her in whatever she may require from you, for she has been a benefactor of many and of myself as well.*

³*Greet Prisca and Aquila, who work with me in Christ Jesus, ⁴and who risked their necks for my life, to whom not only I give thanks, but also all the churches of the Gentiles. ⁵Greet also the church in their house. Greet my beloved Epaenetus, who was the first convert in Asia for Christ. ⁶Greet Mary, who has worked very hard among you. ⁷Greet Andronicus and Junia, my relatives who were in prison with me; they are prominent among the apostles, and they were in Christ before I was. ⁸Greet Ampliatus, my beloved in the Lord. ⁹Greet Urbanus, our co-worker in Christ, and my beloved Stachys. ¹⁰Greet Apelles, who is approved in Christ. Greet those who belong to the family of Aristobulus. ¹¹Greet my relative Herodion. Greet those in the Lord who belong to the family of Narcissus. ¹²Greet those workers in the Lord, Tryphaena and Tryphosa. Greet the beloved Persis, who has worked hard in the Lord. ¹³Greet Rufus, chosen in the Lord; and greet his mother—a mother to me also. ¹⁴Greet Asyncritus, Phlegon, Hermes, Patrobas, Hermas, and the brothers and sisters who are with them. ¹⁵Greet Philologus, Julia, Nereus and his sister, and Olympas, and all the saints who are with them. ¹⁶Greet one another with a holy kiss. All the churches of Christ greet you.*

Although these verses of Paul's letter seem to be simply a series of greeting to no less than twenty-six people, they shed light on the solidarity, composition, and structures of the early church. The first person named is not in Rome but in Cenchreae, the eastern port of Corinth, from which we suppose Paul has written this letter. Phoebe is "a deacon of the church at Cenchreae," exercising the ministry of service in an officially recognized capacity. She has been a "benefactor" to Paul and many others—a wealthy person, putting her private means at public disposal (verses 1–2). She is most probably traveling to Rome on her own business, and for that reason, Paul entrusts to her the delivery of this, his longest and most remarkable letter. Since the reception of Paul's writing was dependent on the impression Phoebe would make on the Christian community of Rome, Paul requests that she be welcomed with the generous hospitality befitting a fellow Christian, "as is fitting for the saints."

For most of the people to whom Paul sends greetings, he adds some other designations. Highlighting Prisca and Aquila, he notes that they worked with him and risked their lives for his (verses 3–4). He identifies Epaenetus as "the first convert in Asia for Christ" (verse 5); Andronicus and Junia as those "who were in prison with me" (verse 7); and Ampliatus as "my beloved in the Lord" (verse 8). Obviously, Paul is joined by an affectionate bond with the Christians of faraway Rome, a bond he longed to see shared among the believers of different backgrounds in the city.

The list also shows Paul referring to the various house churches in the city: the church that meets in the house of Prisca and Aquila (verse 5), those who belong to the "families" of Aristobulus and Narcissus (verses 10–11), the "brothers and sisters" who are with Asyncritus and the others (verse 14), and "all the saints" who are with Philologus and the others (verse 15). Before the days of churches as buildings, Christian gatherings for worship were held in houses, forming the basic cells of Christian community. In the larger cities, the community of believers consisted of a collection of these house churches.

The names indicate a diverse gathering of Gentiles and Jews, wealthy and slaves, women and men. There are Jewish, Greek, and Latin names. A few names are associated with the noble classes but many others are names of slaves or freed persons. Fully one third of the people in Paul's list are women. In addition to Phoebe, there are Prisca, Mary, Junia, Tryphaena and Tryphosa, Persis, the mother of Rufus, Julia, and the sister of Nereus. The fact that women bear half of the designations expressing ministries and roles of service testifies to the abundant apostolic activity of women in the early church.

Paul's list in not a collection of faceless names. Each is a unique member of the Christian community, people who are known and valued. The names remind us that Paul's letter was not an abstract theology. It was written to an average cross section of persons in first-century Rome. Paul wrote with these people in mind, confident that his letter would be understandable and speak to their lives. He urges them all to "greet one another with a holy kiss" (verse 16). Through this gesture, members of the church communicated to one another a sense of the love and unity distinctive of Christian life. The ritual of the "kiss of peace" became a key feature of Christian liturgy very early on. Within the church's gathering on the Lord's Day, the kiss was both a reminder and expression of that unity for which Paul so longed for the church. Finally, Paul adds, "All the churches of Christ greet you," by which he includes himself and the other churches he serves in the exchange of peace. In this gesture, Paul inserts himself right into the community in Rome gathered to hear his letter. He ensures that each person will feel personally greeted by him.

Reflection and Discussion

- What do Paul's greetings tell us about Paul's awareness of this church he had never visited?

- Concerning Phoebe, Paul urges the Christians in Rome to "welcome her in the Lord as is fitting for the saints." What does this indicate about how a church should welcome a visitor?

- In the church's transition from house churches to basilicas, what have we lost and what have we gained?

- What do I find most remarkable about Paul's greetings to the saints in Rome?

Prayer

Risen Lord, you formed your church on the foundation of the apostles, and you call each person to some form of ministry and service. Help me live out my calling as your disciple and as a member of your church.

I want you to be wise in what is good and guileless in what is evil. The God of peace will shortly crush Satan under your feet. The grace of our Lord Jesus Christ be with you.
ROMANS 16:19–20

Final Advice and Prayer

ROMANS 16:17–27 [17]*I urge you, brothers and sisters, to keep an eye on those who cause dissensions and offenses, in opposition to the teaching that you have learned; avoid them.* [18]*For such people do not serve our Lord Christ, but their own appetites, and by smooth talk and flattery they deceive the hearts of the simple-minded.* [19]*For while your obedience is known to all, so that I rejoice over you, I want you to be wise in what is good and guileless in what is evil.* [20]*The God of peace will shortly crush Satan under your feet. The grace of our Lord Jesus Christ be with you.*

[21]*Timothy, my co-worker, greets you; so do Lucius and Jason and Sosipater, my relatives.*

[22]*I Tertius, the writer of this letter, greet you in the Lord.*

[23]*Gaius, who is host to me and to the whole church, greets you. Erastus, the city treasurer, and our brother Quartus, greet you.*

[25]*Now to God who is able to strengthen you according to my gospel and the proclamation of Jesus Christ, according to the revelation of the mystery that was kept secret for long ages* [26]*but is now disclosed, and through the prophetic writings is made known to all the Gentiles, according to the command of the eternal God, to bring about the obedience of faith—*[27]*to the only wise God, through Jesus Christ, to whom be the glory forever! Amen.*

Because Paul understands that there is an ever-present danger of false teaching in the church, he adds a final word of advice, urging his hearers to beware of "those who cause dissensions and offenses" (verse 17). The standard for detecting these errors, Paul says, is that false teaching is "in opposition to the teaching that you have learned." All of his letters indicate the necessity of passing on the tradition that comes from Christ and the apostles, exhorting his readers to trust in the church's apostolic teachers.

Despite appearances of piety, false teachers do not serve Jesus Christ, but "their own appetites" (verse 18). Through their hunger for recognition, celebrity, money, influence, or other selfish interests, they betray the gospel. With their "smooth talk and flattery," they deceive the hearts and minds of God's people. So, Paul implores his listeners, "I want you to be wise in what is good and guileless in what is evil" (verse 19). That is, in the context of people of good will, seek to be discerning; but, in the context of a smooth-talking deceiver, pursue innocence. This proverbial saying is similar to the words of Jesus when he was instructing his disciples about the dangers awaiting them in the mission field: "See, I am sending you out like sheep into the midst of wolves; so be wise as serpents and innocent as doves" (Matt 10:16).

Paul's warning ends on a note of confidence in God's deliverance: "The God of peace will shortly crush Satan under your feet" (verse 20). Like a defeated enemy, the Evil One will be crushed under the feet of God's people. But the victory comes only through "the grace of our Lord Jesus Christ." As a sign of solidarity in battle, Paul adds greetings from his associates, some of whom may be preparing to accompany Paul to Jerusalem. Among these are Timothy, Paul's co-worker mentioned in many of Paul's letters, and Tertius, who penned the letter as Paul dictated it (verses 21–22). Gaius, who hosts the Corinthian community in his house church, and other members of the church there add their greetings (verse 23).

The closing prayer nicely connects the end of the letter with its beginning, focusing on the gospel of Jesus Christ as proclaimed by Paul, promised through the prophets of the ancient Scriptures, and summoning all the Gentiles to the obedience of faith (verses 25–27; Rom 1:1–6). The "mystery" that was kept secret for long ages, the plan of God for drawing the world back into his saving embrace, is now revealed in this messianic age. Although the Old Testament writings heralded the gospel, they remained opaque until now. But when a person comes to faith in Israel's Messiah, the Spirit removes the veil to reveal the pattern of God's saving work as it converged on the death and resurrection of Jesus Christ. The new eyes attained through faith enable believers to see how God has brought blessings to all nations through the mercy and faithfulness embodied in Jesus Christ.

Shortly after dictating his letter, Paul set off for Jerusalem, in the hopes of then visiting Rome on his way to Spain. But, as we know from the final chapters of the Acts of the Apostles, Paul's visit to Jerusalem was disastrous, involving riots, beatings, trials, and imprisonment. And he did later arrive in Rome, not as a daring missionary but as a prisoner in chains. His story in Acts ends, after a perilous sea voyage and shipwreck, as a prisoner awaiting trial before Caesar's tribunal. Whether Paul ever made it to Spain we do not know. Paul was killed at the hands of the Emperor Nero, beheaded and buried outside the Roman city walls. He died as he had lived—a faithful witness to the gospel, spending his life for the salvation of all people.

Reflection and Discussion

- How do I discern the difference between truly false teaching and a teaching that happens not to coincide with the way I am used to hearing a matter spoken about?

- What are the characteristics of false teachers? In what ways do they serve "their own appetites" rather than Christ?

- Do I have a group of companions in Christ who have labored and suffered with me? What does it mean to be a co-worker with another in the Christian life?

- What has Paul taught me in his Letter to the Romans about being a missionary disciple of Jesus?

Prayer

Lord Jesus Christ, with gratitude to your apostle Paul, I pray for missionaries who preach the gospel, especially where it crosses cultural boundaries. May the good news of God's kingdom bring harmony and reconciliation to all people.

SUGGESTIONS FOR FACILITATORS, GROUP SESSION 6

1. Welcome group members and make any final announcements or requests.

2. You may want to pray this prayer as a group:

   God of Peace, who has reconciled Jews and Gentiles and joined them together as your people, may we live in harmony with our brothers and sisters in Christ, so that we may glorify you with one voice. Guide our choices so that we may use our newfound freedom well, setting priorities rightly, serving as an example to others, and building up your church. May we build bridges and tear down walls so that the good news of your kingdom may bring justice, solidarity, and reconciliation to all people.

3. Ask one or more of the following questions:
   - How has this study of the Letter to the Romans enriched your life?
   - In what way has this study challenged you the most?

4. Discuss lessons 25 through 30. Choose one or more of the questions for reflection and discussion from each lesson to discuss as a group.

5. Ask the group if they would like to study another in the Threshold Bible Study series. Discuss the topic and dates, and make a decision among those interested. Ask the group members to suggest people they would like to invite to participate in the next study series.

6. Ask the group to discuss the insights that stand out most from this study over the past six weeks.

7. Conclude by praying aloud the following prayer or another of your own choosing:

   Holy Spirit of the living God, you inspired the writers of the Scriptures and you have guided our study during these weeks. Continue to deepen our love for the word of God in the holy Scriptures, and draw us more deeply into the heart of Jesus. We thank you for the confident hope you have placed within us and the gifts that build up the church. Through this study, lead us to worship and witness more fully and fervently, and bless us now and always with the fire of your love.

Ordering Additional Studies

AVAILABLE TITLES IN THIS SERIES INCLUDE...

Advent Light

Angels of God

Divine Mercy

Eucharist

The Feasts of Judaism

God's Spousal Love

The Holy Spirit and Spiritual Gifts

Jerusalem, the Holy City

Missionary Discipleship

Mysteries of the Rosary

The Names of Jesus

People of the Passion

Pilgrimage in the Footsteps of Jesus

The Resurrection and the Life

The Sacred Heart of Jesus

Salvation Offered to All People

Stewardship of the Earth

The Tragic and Triumphant Cross

Jesus, the Messianic King
(Part 1): Matthew 1–16

Jesus, the Messianic King
(Part 2): Matthew 17–28

Jesus, the Word Made Flesh
(Part 1): John 1–10

Jesus, the Word Made Flesh
(Part 2): John 11–21

Jesus, the Suffering Servant
(Part 1): Mark 1–8

Jesus, the Suffering Servant
(Part 2): Mark 9–16

Jesus, the Compassionate Savior
(Part 1): Luke 1–11

Jesus, the Compassionate Savior
(Part 2): Luke 12–24

Church of the Holy Spirit
(Part 1): Acts of the Apostles 1–14

Church of the Holy Spirit
(Part 2): Acts of the Apostles 15–28

The Lamb and the Beasts:
The Book of Revelation

TWENTY-THIRD
PUBLICATIONS

TO CHECK AVAILABILITY OR FOR A DESCRIPTION
OF EACH STUDY, VISIT OUR WEBSITE AT
www.ThresholdBibleStudy.com
OR CALL US AT 1-800-321-0411